Magical History Tour

FIRST STEPS ON THE MOON
The Apollo Project

FABRICE ERRE
Writer

SYLVAIN SAVOIA
Artist

NEW YORK

Magical History Tour

#10 "First Steps on the Moon: The Apollo Project"

By Fabrice Erre and Sylvain Savoia

Original series editors: Frédéric Niffle and Lewis Trondheim
Translation: Nanette McGuinness

Mark McNabb – Production
Wilson Ramos Jr – Letterer
Zachary Harris — Editorial Intern
Stephanie Brooks — Assistant Managing Editor
Jim Salicrup
Editor-in-Chief

ISBN 978-1-5458-0894-8

Papercutz books may be purchased for business or promotional use. For information on bulk purchases, please contact Macmillan Corporate and Premium Sales Department at (800) 221-7945 x5442.

Printed in Malaysia
August 2022

Distributed by Macmillan
First Papercutz Printing

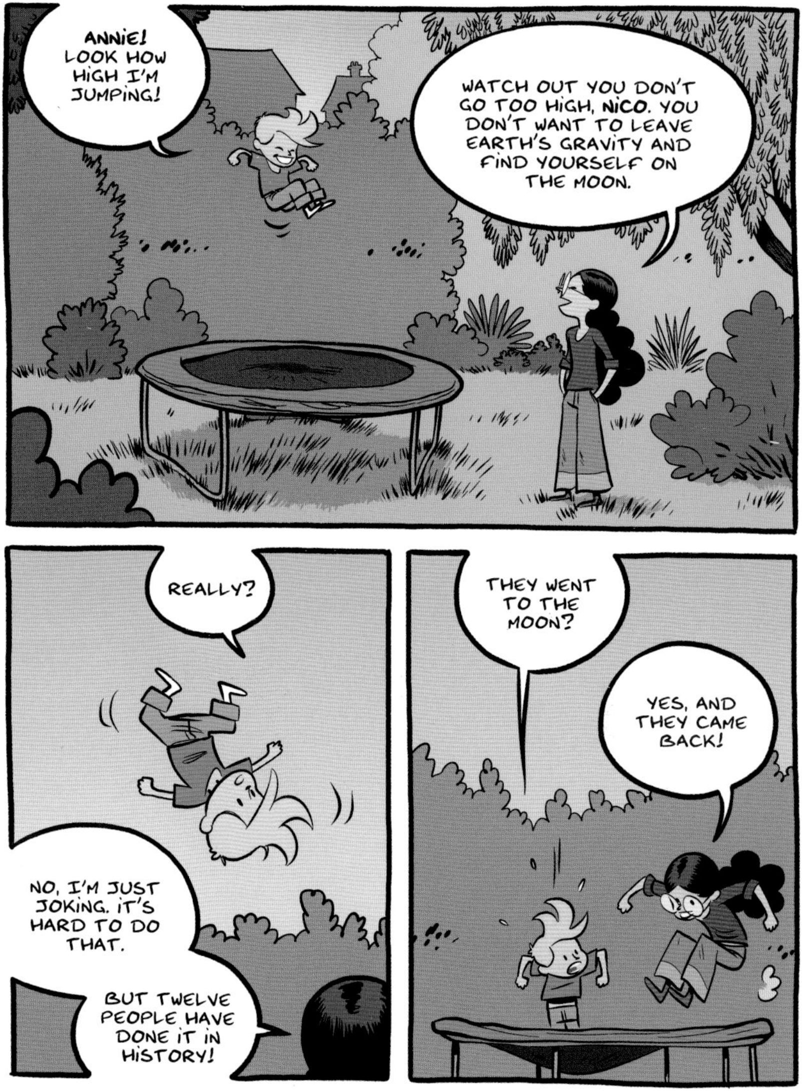
ANNIE! LOOK HOW HIGH I'M JUMPING!
WATCH OUT YOU DON'T GO TOO HIGH, NICO. YOU DON'T WANT TO LEAVE EARTH'S GRAVITY AND FIND YOURSELF ON THE MOON.
REALLY?
NO, I'M JUST JOKING. IT'S HARD TO DO THAT.
BUT TWELVE PEOPLE HAVE DONE IT IN HISTORY!
THEY WENT TO THE MOON?
YES, AND THEY CAME BACK!

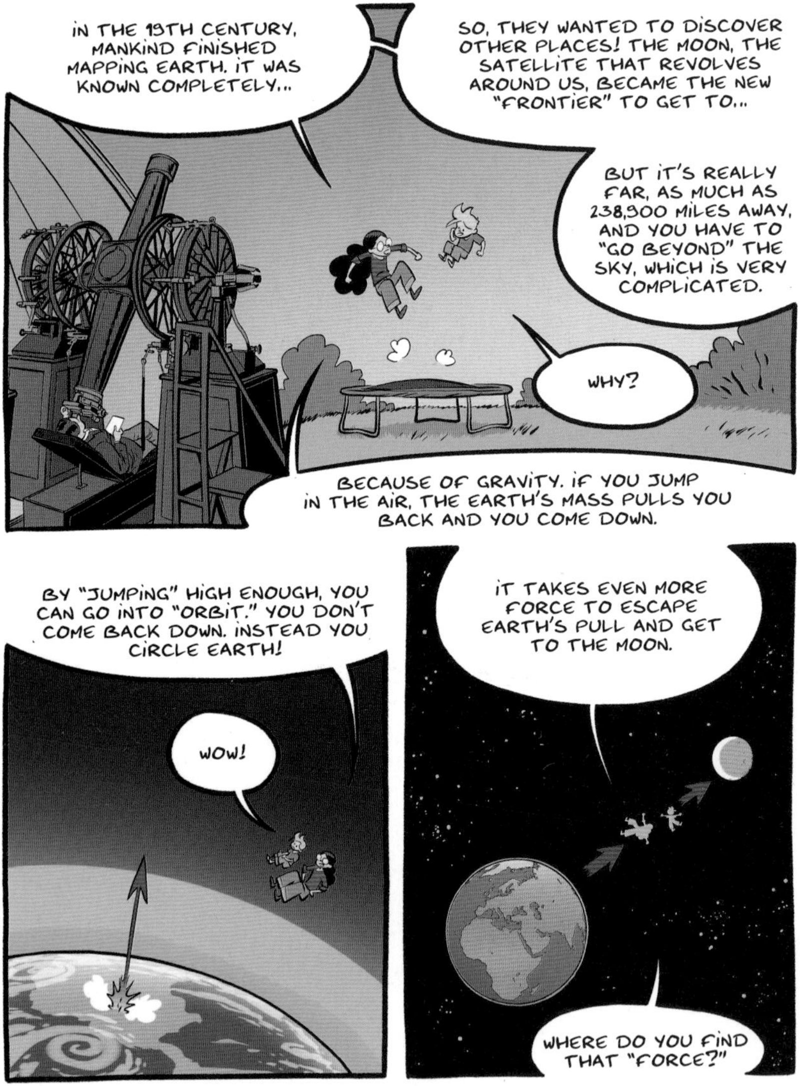
IN THE 19TH CENTURY, MANKIND FINISHED MAPPING EARTH. IT WAS KNOWN COMPLETELY...
SO, THEY WANTED TO DISCOVER OTHER PLACES! THE MOON, THE SATELLITE THAT REVOLVES AROUND US, BECAME THE NEW "FRONTIER" TO GET TO...
BUT IT'S REALLY FAR, AS MUCH AS 238,900 MILES AWAY, AND YOU HAVE TO "GO BEYOND" THE SKY, WHICH IS VERY COMPLICATED.
WHY?
BECAUSE OF GRAVITY. IF YOU JUMP IN THE AIR, THE EARTH'S MASS PULLS YOU BACK AND YOU COME DOWN.
BY "JUMPING" HIGH ENOUGH, YOU CAN GO INTO "ORBIT." YOU DON'T COME BACK DOWN. INSTEAD YOU CIRCLE EARTH!
WOW!
IT TAKES EVEN MORE FORCE TO ESCAPE EARTH'S PULL AND GET TO THE MOON.
WHERE DO YOU FIND THAT "FORCE?"

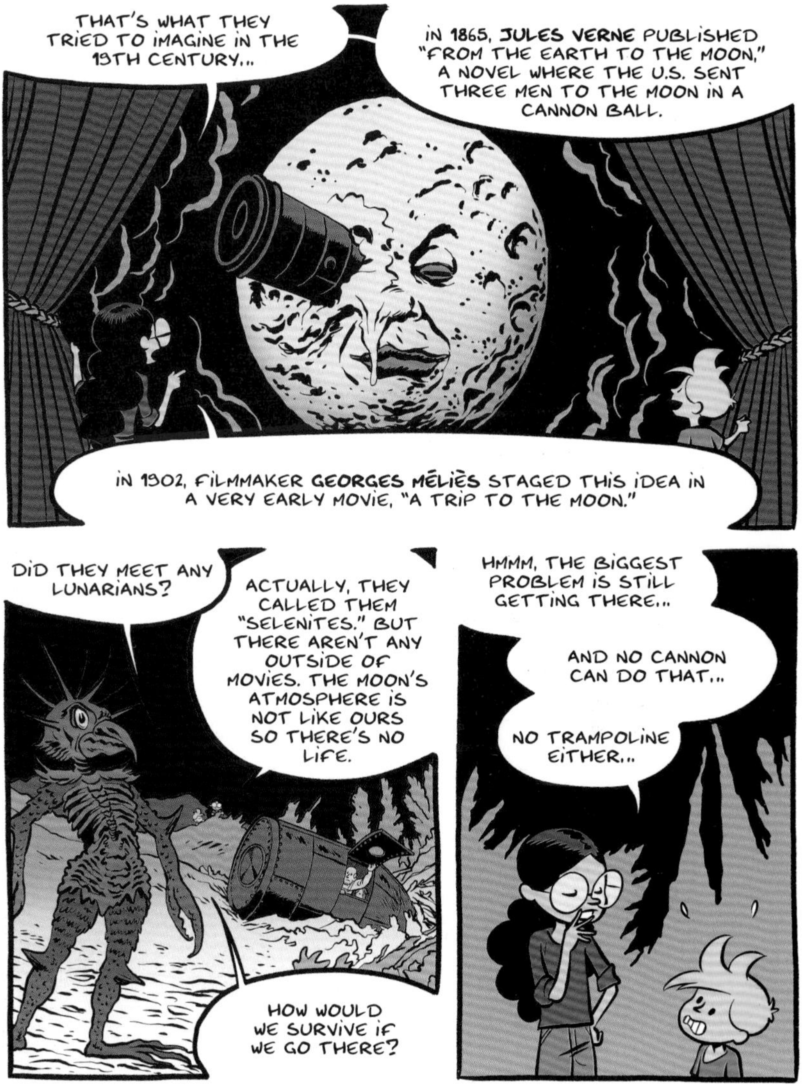
THAT'S WHAT THEY TRIED TO IMAGINE IN THE 19TH CENTURY...
IN 1865, JULES VERNE PUBLISHED "FROM THE EARTH TO THE MOON," A NOVEL WHERE THE U.S. SENT THREE MEN TO THE MOON IN A CANNON BALL.
IN 1902, FILMMAKER GEORGES MÉLIÈS STAGED THIS IDEA IN A VERY EARLY MOVIE, "A TRIP TO THE MOON."
DID THEY MEET ANY LUNARIANS?
ACTUALLY, THEY CALLED THEM "SELENITES." BUT THERE AREN'T ANY OUTSIDE OF MOVIES. THE MOON'S ATMOSPHERE IS NOT LIKE OURS SO THERE'S NO LIFE.
HOW WOULD WE SURVIVE IF WE GO THERE?
HMMM, THE BIGGEST PROBLEM IS STILL GETTING THERE...
AND NO CANNON CAN DO THAT...
NO TRAMPOLINE EITHER...

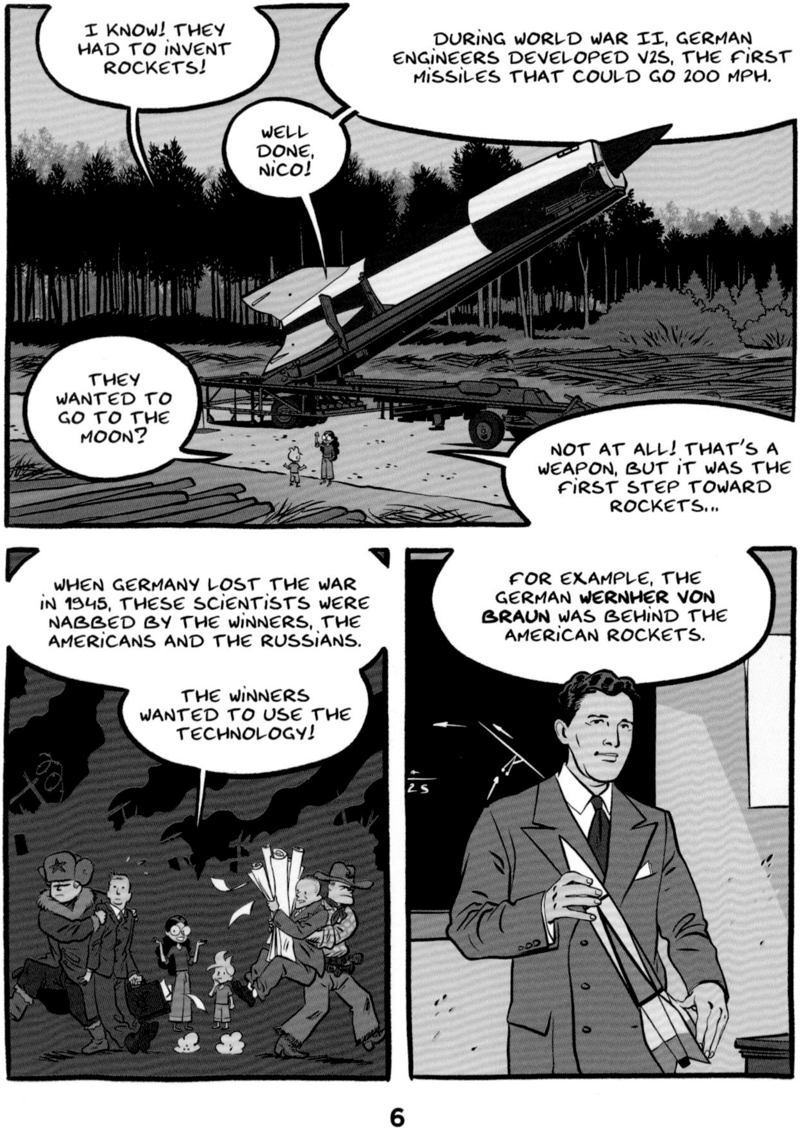
I KNOW! THEY HAD TO INVENT ROCKETS!
DURING WORLD WAR II, GERMAN ENGINEERS DEVELOPED V2S, THE FIRST MISSILES THAT COULD GO 200 MPH.
WELL DONE, NICO!
THEY WANTED TO GO TO THE MOON?
NOT AT ALL! THAT'S A WEAPON, BUT IT WAS THE FIRST STEP TOWARD ROCKETS...
WHEN GERMANY LOST THE WAR IN 1945, THESE SCIENTISTS WERE NABBED BY THE WINNERS, THE AMERICANS AND THE RUSSIANS.
THE WINNERS WANTED TO USE THE TECHNOLOGY!
FOR EXAMPLE, THE GERMAN **WERNHER VON BRAUN** WAS BEHIND THE AMERICAN ROCKETS.

THE 1950S-60S WERE CHARACTERIZED BY THE RIVALRY BETWEEN THE UNITED STATES AND THE U.S.S.R. (RUSSIA), WHICH WE CALLED THE "COLD WAR."

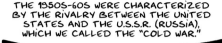

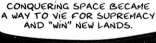

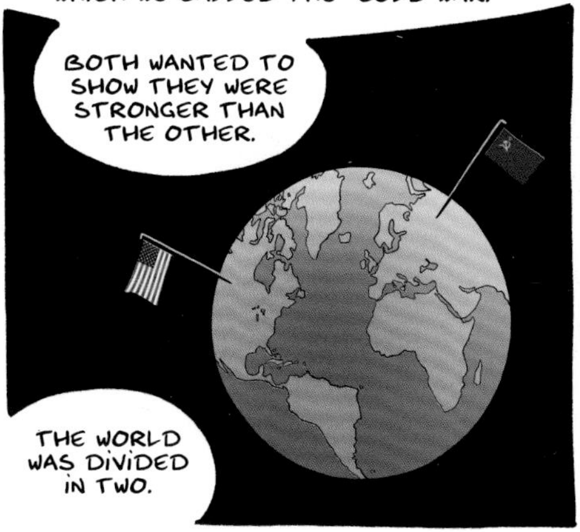
BOTH WANTED TO SHOW THEY WERE STRONGER THAN THE OTHER.
THE WORLD WAS DIVIDED IN TWO.

CONQUERING SPACE BECAME A WAY TO VIE FOR SUPREMACY AND "WIN" NEW LANDS.

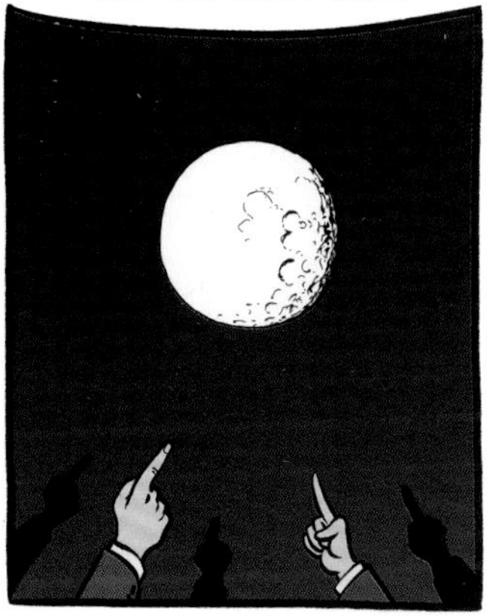

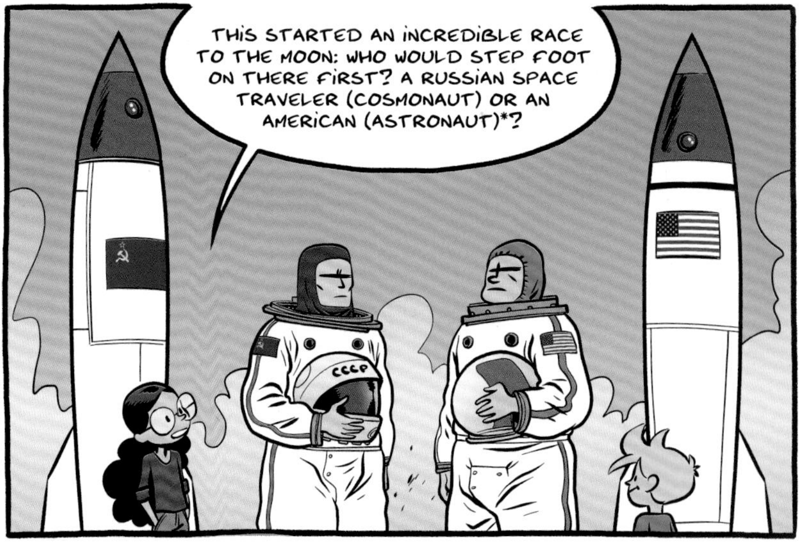
THIS STARTED AN INCREDIBLE RACE TO THE MOON: WHO WOULD STEP FOOT ON THERE FIRST? A RUSSIAN SPACE TRAVELER (COSMONAUT) OR AN AMERICAN (ASTRONAUT)*?
CCCP

*THESE WORDS COME FROM THE GREEK: "KOSMOS" (UNIVERSE), "ASTRON" (STARS), AND "NAUTES" (SEAFARER).

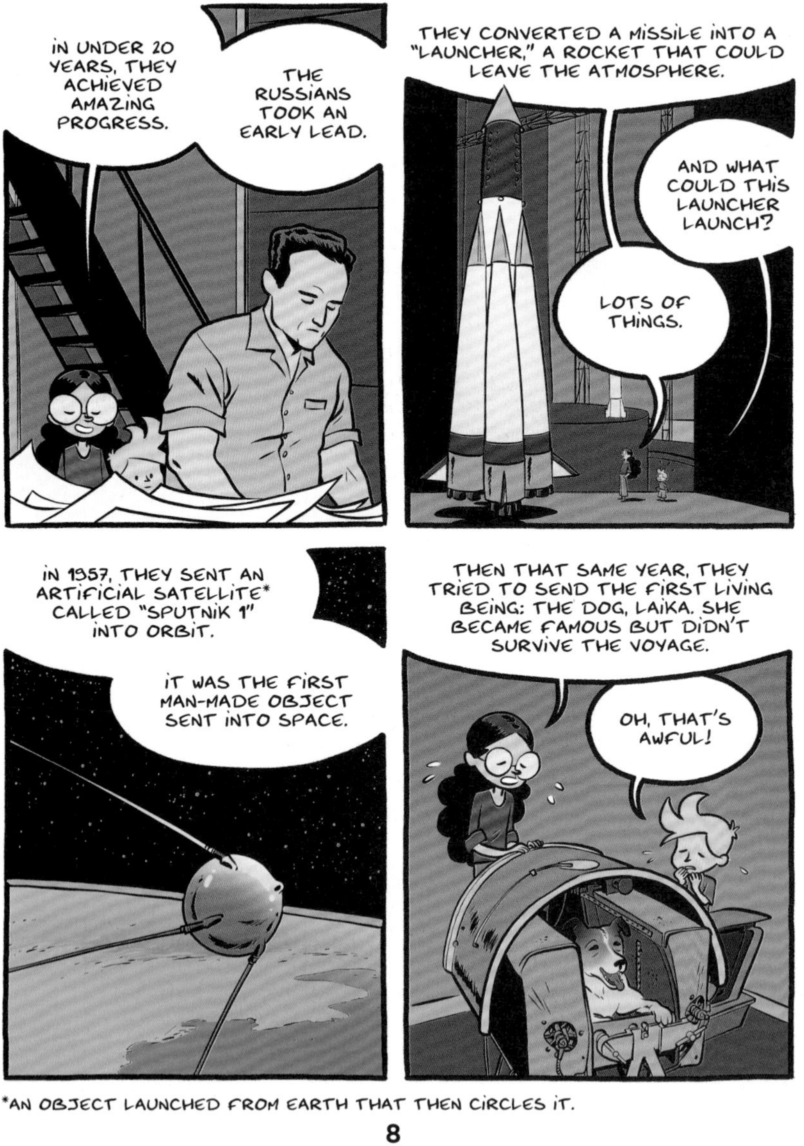
IN UNDER 20 YEARS, THEY ACHIEVED AMAZING PROGRESS.
THE RUSSIANS TOOK AN EARLY LEAD.
THEY CONVERTED A MISSILE INTO A "LAUNCHER," A ROCKET THAT COULD LEAVE THE ATMOSPHERE.
AND WHAT COULD THIS LAUNCHER LAUNCH?
LOTS OF THINGS.
IN 1957, THEY SENT AN ARTIFICIAL SATELLITE* CALLED "SPUTNIK 1" INTO ORBIT.
IT WAS THE FIRST MAN-MADE OBJECT SENT INTO SPACE.
THEN THAT SAME YEAR, THEY TRIED TO SEND THE FIRST LIVING BEING: THE DOG, LAIKA. SHE BECAME FAMOUS BUT DIDN'T SURVIVE THE VOYAGE.
OH, THAT'S AWFUL!

*AN OBJECT LAUNCHED FROM EARTH THAT THEN CIRCLES IT.

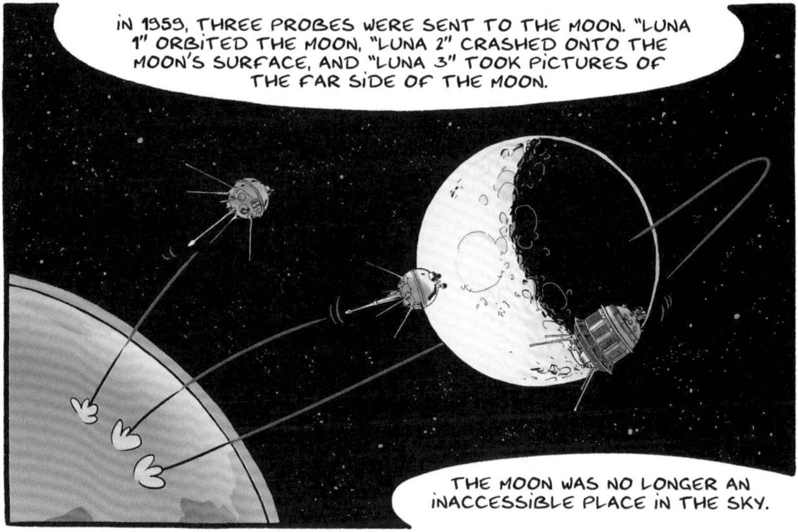
IN 1959, THREE PROBES WERE SENT TO THE MOON. "LUNA 1" ORBITED THE MOON, "LUNA 2" CRASHED ONTO THE MOON'S SURFACE, AND "LUNA 3" TOOK PICTURES OF THE FAR SIDE OF THE MOON.
THE MOON WAS NO LONGER AN INACCESSIBLE PLACE IN THE SKY.

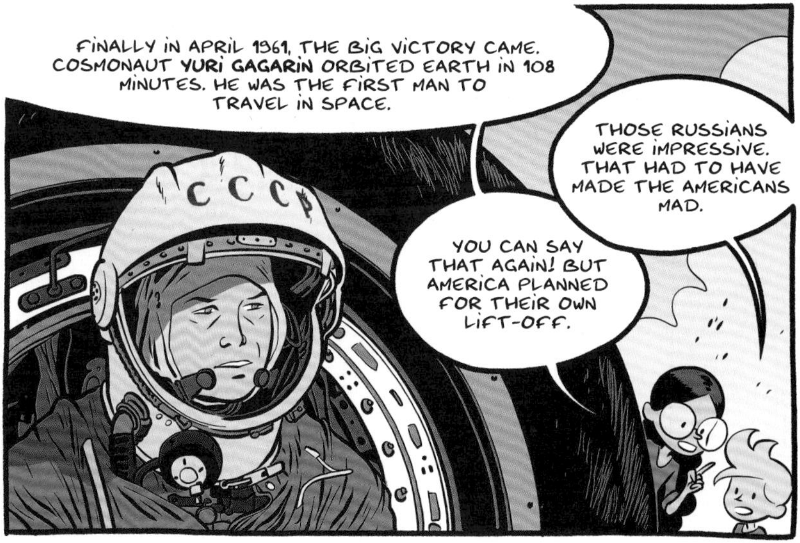
FINALLY IN APRIL 1961, THE BIG VICTORY CAME. COSMONAUT YURI GAGARIN ORBITED EARTH IN 108 MINUTES. HE WAS THE FIRST MAN TO TRAVEL IN SPACE.
CCCP
THOSE RUSSIANS WERE IMPRESSIVE. THAT HAD TO HAVE MADE THE AMERICANS MAD.
YOU CAN SAY THAT AGAIN! BUT AMERICA PLANNED FOR THEIR OWN LIFT-OFF.

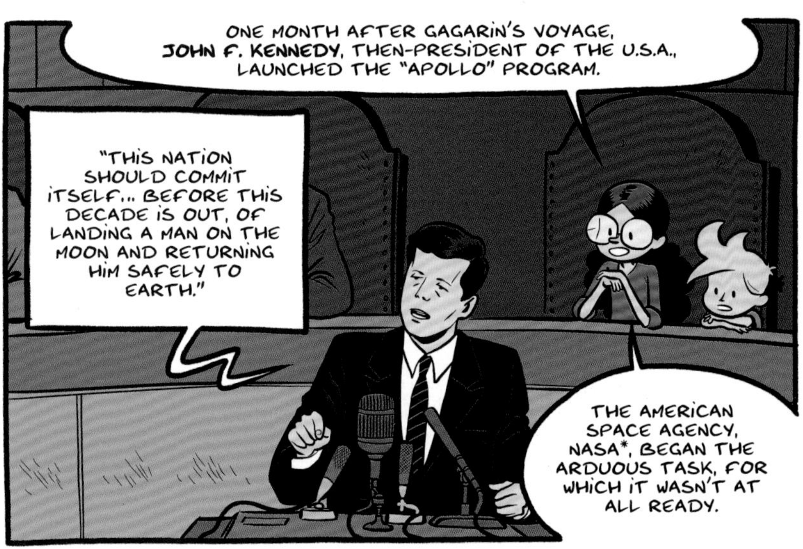
ONE MONTH AFTER GAGARIN'S VOYAGE, JOHN F. KENNEDY, THEN-PRESIDENT OF THE U.S.A., LAUNCHED THE "APOLLO" PROGRAM.
"THIS NATION SHOULD COMMIT ITSELF... BEFORE THIS DECADE IS OUT, OF LANDING A MAN ON THE MOON AND RETURNING HIM SAFELY TO EARTH."
THE AMERICAN SPACE AGENCY, NASA*, BEGAN THE ARDUOUS TASK, FOR WHICH IT WASN'T AT ALL READY.

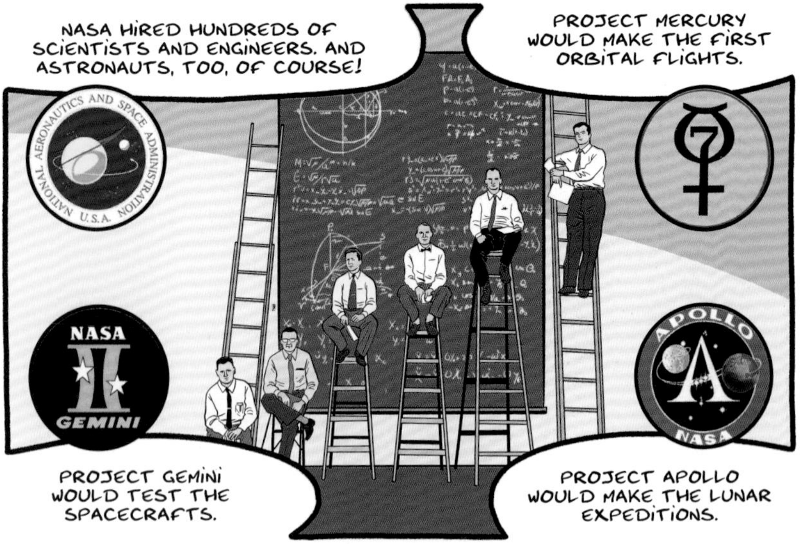
NASA HIRED HUNDREDS OF SCIENTISTS AND ENGINEERS. AND ASTRONAUTS, TOO, OF COURSE!
PROJECT MERCURY WOULD MAKE THE FIRST ORBITAL FLIGHTS.
NATIONAL AERONAUTICS AND SPACE ADMINISTRATION U.S.A.
NASA
GEMINI
APOLLO
NASA
PROJECT GEMINI WOULD TEST THE SPACECRAFTS.
PROJECT APOLLO WOULD MAKE THE LUNAR EXPEDITIONS.

*NATIONAL AERONAUTICS AND SPACE ADMINISTRATION

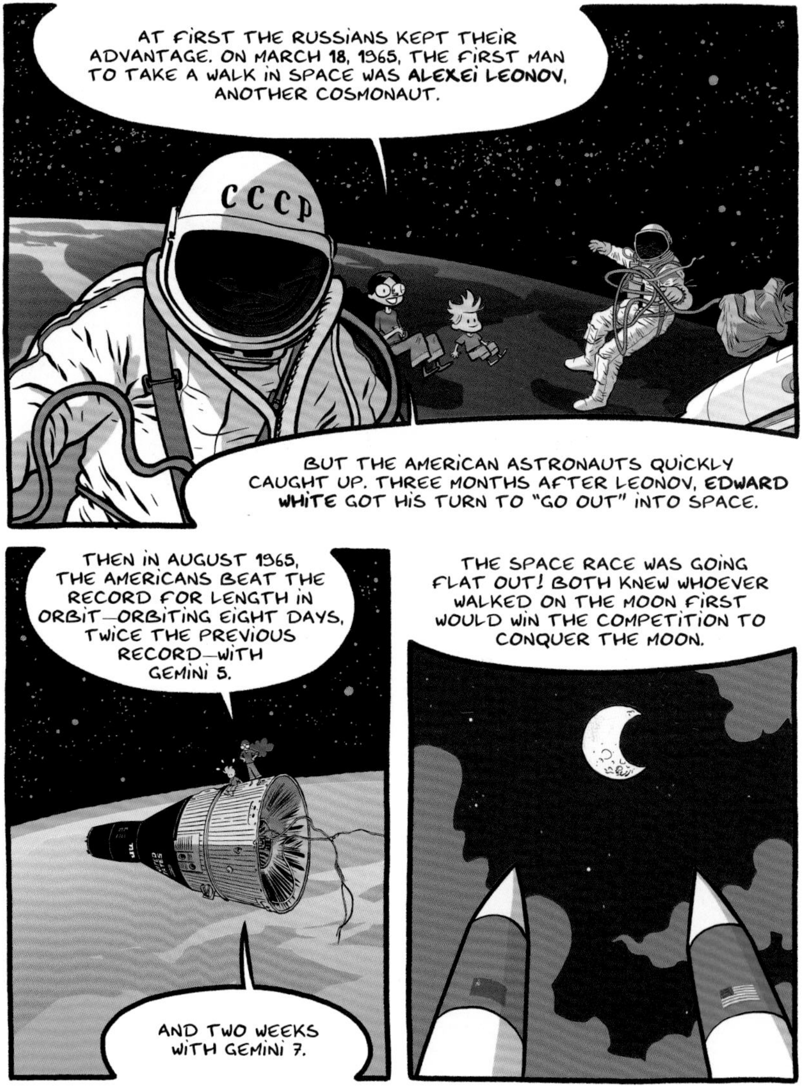
AT FIRST THE RUSSIANS KEPT THEIR ADVANTAGE. ON MARCH 18, 1965, THE FIRST MAN TO TAKE A WALK IN SPACE WAS **ALEXEI LEONOV**, ANOTHER COSMONAUT.
CCCP
BUT THE AMERICAN ASTRONAUTS QUICKLY CAUGHT UP. THREE MONTHS AFTER LEONOV, **EDWARD WHITE** GOT HIS TURN TO "GO OUT" INTO SPACE.
THEN IN AUGUST 1965, THE AMERICANS BEAT THE RECORD FOR LENGTH IN ORBIT—ORBITING EIGHT DAYS, TWICE THE PREVIOUS RECORD—WITH GEMINI 5.
AND TWO WEEKS WITH GEMINI 7.
THE SPACE RACE WAS GOING FLAT OUT! BOTH KNEW WHOEVER WALKED ON THE MOON FIRST WOULD WIN THE COMPETITION TO CONQUER THE MOON.

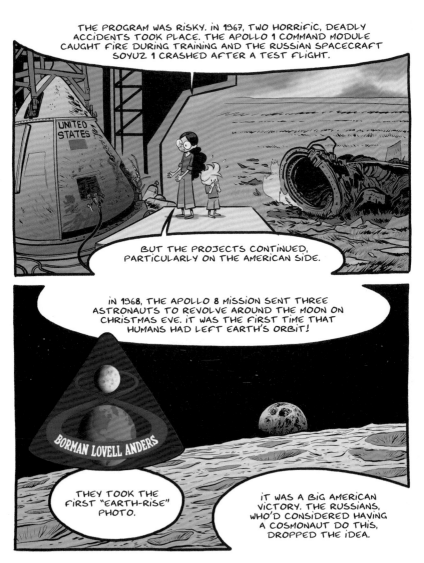

THE PROGRAM WAS RISKY. IN 1967, TWO HORRIFIC, DEADLY ACCIDENTS TOOK PLACE. THE APOLLO 1 COMMAND MODULE CAUGHT FIRE DURING TRAINING AND THE RUSSIAN SPACECRAFT SOYUZ 1 CRASHED AFTER A TEST FLIGHT.

UNITED STATES

BUT THE PROJECTS CONTINUED, PARTICULARLY ON THE AMERICAN SIDE.

IN 1968, THE APOLLO 8 MISSION SENT THREE ASTRONAUTS TO REVOLVE AROUND THE MOON ON CHRISTMAS EVE. IT WAS THE FIRST TIME THAT HUMANS HAD LEFT EARTH'S ORBIT!

BORMAN LOVELL ANDERS

THEY TOOK THE FIRST "EARTH-RISE" PHOTO.

IT WAS A BIG AMERICAN VICTORY. THE RUSSIANS, WHO'D CONSIDERED HAVING A COSMONAUT DO THIS, DROPPED THE IDEA.

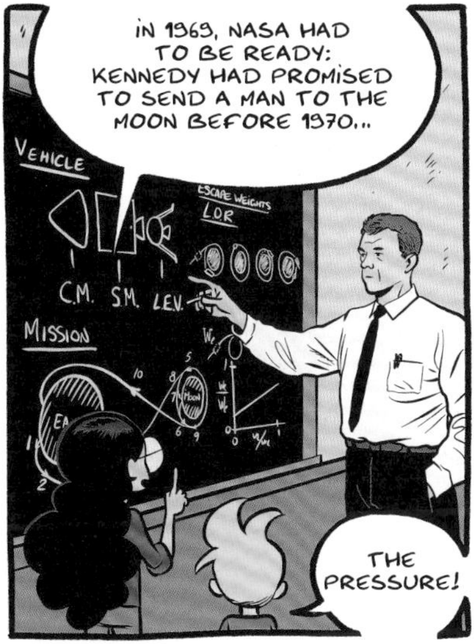
IN 1969, NASA HAD TO BE READY: KENNEDY HAD PROMISED TO SEND A MAN TO THE MOON BEFORE 1970...
VEHICLE
ESCAPE WEIGHTS
LOR
C.M.
S.M.
LEV.
MISSION
MOON
THE PRESSURE!

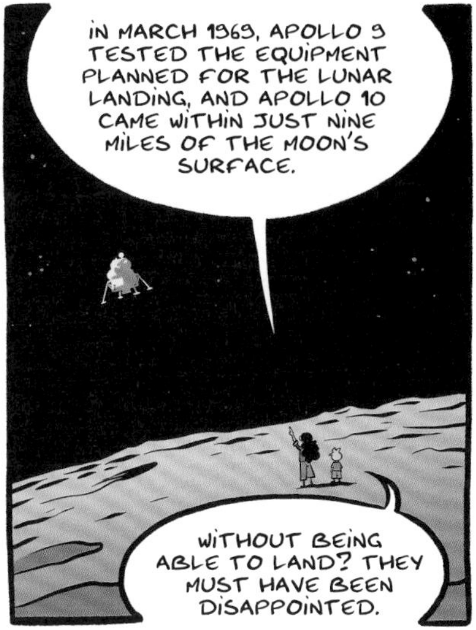
IN MARCH 1969, APOLLO 9 TESTED THE EQUIPMENT PLANNED FOR THE LUNAR LANDING, AND APOLLO 10 CAME WITHIN JUST NINE MILES OF THE MOON'S SURFACE.
WITHOUT BEING ABLE TO LAND? THEY MUST HAVE BEEN DISAPPOINTED.

EACH MISSION HAD VERY PRECISE GOALS. THE ASTRONAUTS COULDN'T JUST DO WHAT THEY WANTED.

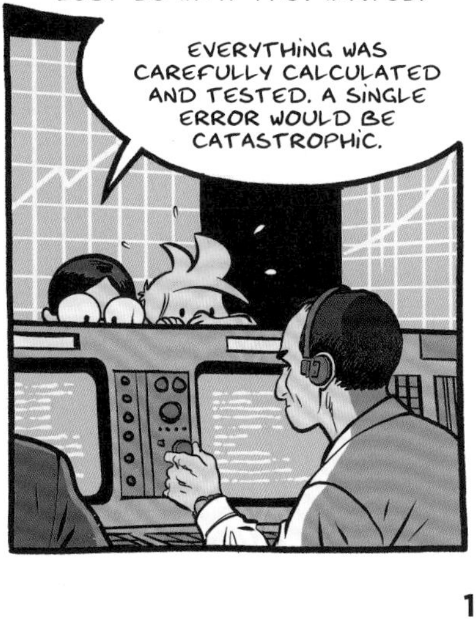
EVERYTHING WAS CAREFULLY CALCULATED AND TESTED. A SINGLE ERROR WOULD BE CATASTROPHIC.

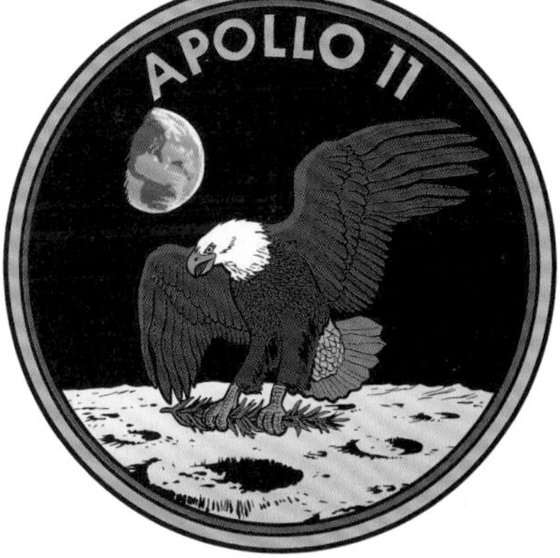
APOLLO 11

DURING THIS TIME, THE APOLLO 11 CREW WAS GETTING READY TO TAKE THE BIG TRIP.

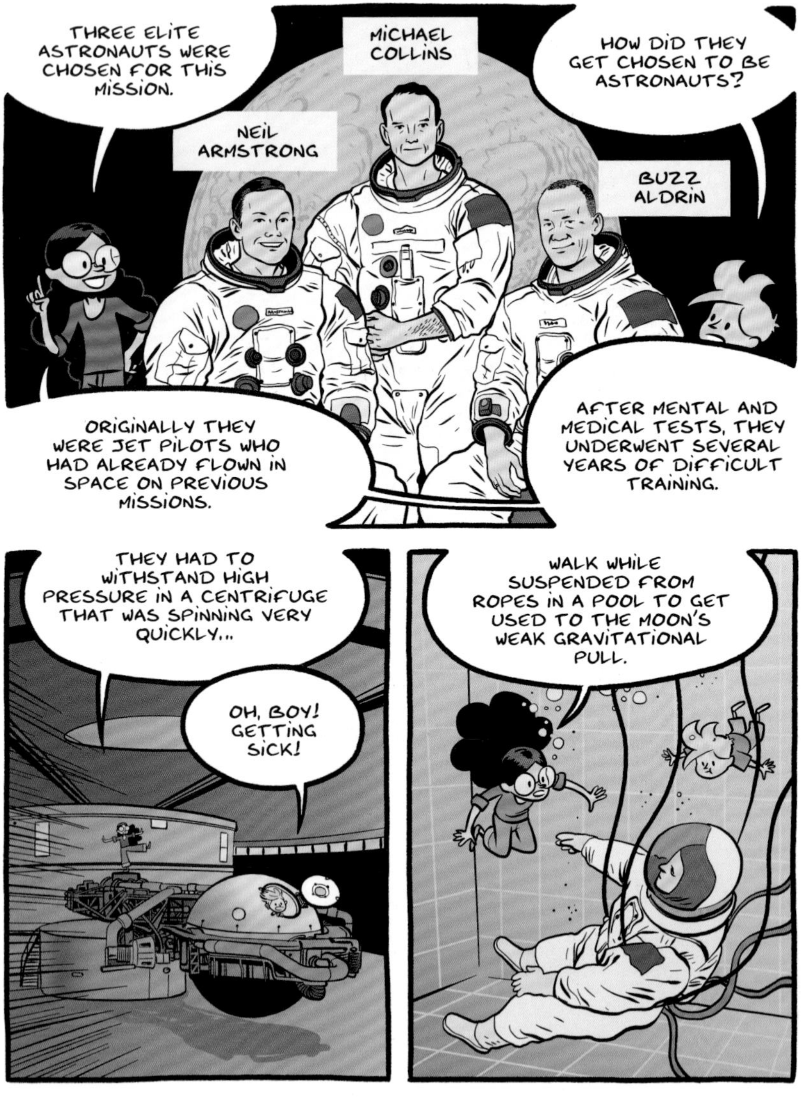
THREE ELITE ASTRONAUTS WERE CHOSEN FOR THIS MISSION.
MICHAEL COLLINS
NEIL ARMSTRONG
BUZZ ALDRIN
HOW DID THEY GET CHOSEN TO BE ASTRONAUTS?
ORIGINALLY THEY WERE JET PILOTS WHO HAD ALREADY FLOWN IN SPACE ON PREVIOUS MISSIONS.
AFTER MENTAL AND MEDICAL TESTS, THEY UNDERWENT SEVERAL YEARS OF DIFFICULT TRAINING.
THEY HAD TO WITHSTAND HIGH PRESSURE IN A CENTRIFUGE THAT WAS SPINNING VERY QUICKLY...
OH, BOY! GETTING SICK!
WALK WHILE SUSPENDED FROM ROPES IN A POOL TO GET USED TO THE MOON'S WEAK GRAVITATIONAL PULL.

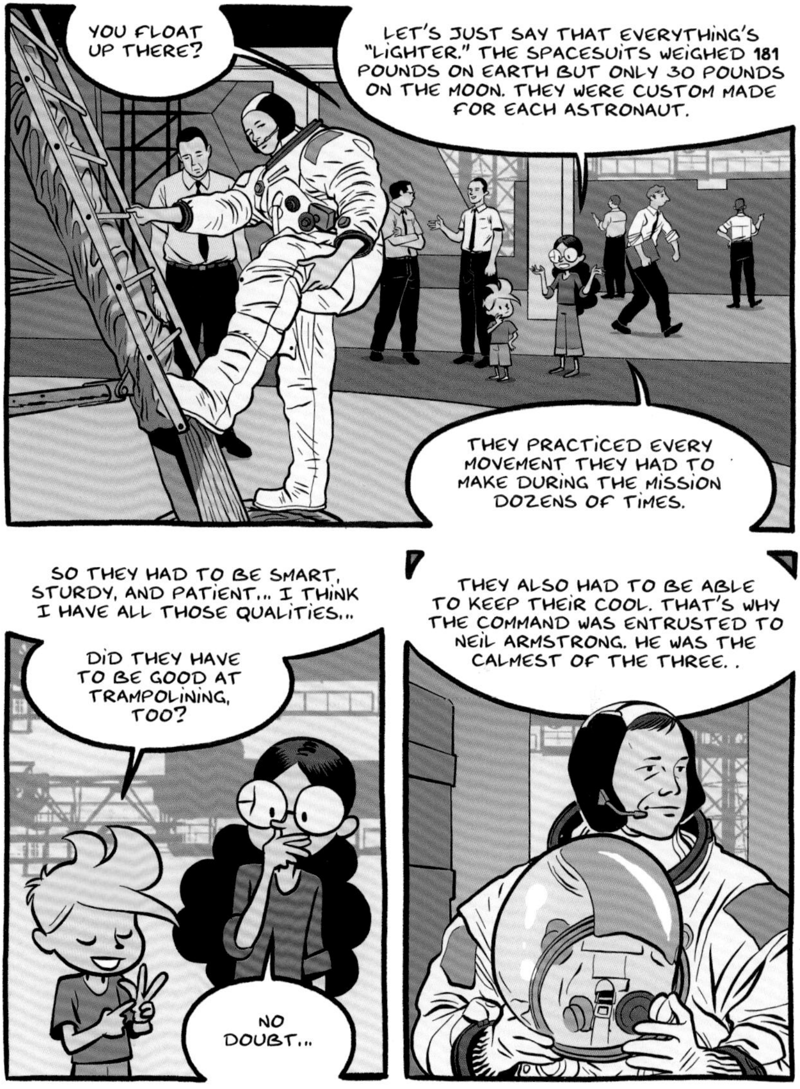
YOU FLOAT UP THERE?
LET'S JUST SAY THAT EVERYTHING'S "LIGHTER." THE SPACESUITS WEIGHED 181 POUNDS ON EARTH BUT ONLY 30 POUNDS ON THE MOON. THEY WERE CUSTOM MADE FOR EACH ASTRONAUT.
THEY PRACTICED EVERY MOVEMENT THEY HAD TO MAKE DURING THE MISSION DOZENS OF TIMES.
SO THEY HAD TO BE SMART, STURDY, AND PATIENT... I THINK I HAVE ALL THOSE QUALITIES...
DID THEY HAVE TO BE GOOD AT TRAMPOLINING, TOO?
NO DOUBT...
THEY ALSO HAD TO BE ABLE TO KEEP THEIR COOL. THAT'S WHY THE COMMAND WAS ENTRUSTED TO NEIL ARMSTRONG. HE WAS THE CALMEST OF THE THREE. .

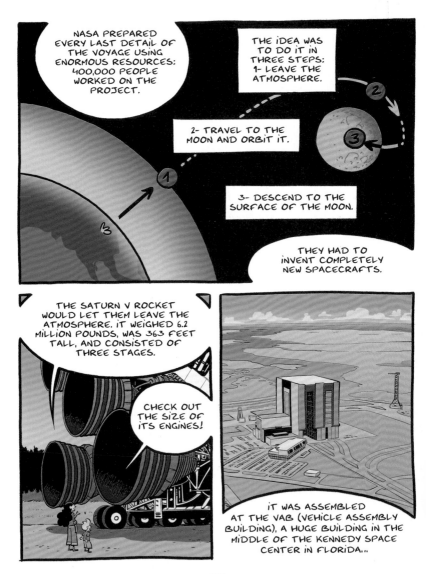

NASA PREPARED EVERY LAST DETAIL OF THE VOYAGE USING ENORMOUS RESOURCES: 400,000 PEOPLE WORKED ON THE PROJECT.

THE IDEA WAS TO DO IT IN THREE STEPS: 1- LEAVE THE ATMOSPHERE.

2- TRAVEL TO THE MOON AND ORBIT IT.

3- DESCEND TO THE SURFACE OF THE MOON.

THEY HAD TO INVENT COMPLETELY NEW SPACECRAFTS.

THE SATURN V ROCKET WOULD LET THEM LEAVE THE ATMOSPHERE. IT WEIGHED 6.2 MILLION POUNDS, WAS 363 FEET TALL, AND CONSISTED OF THREE STAGES.

CHECK OUT THE SIZE OF ITS ENGINES!

IT WAS ASSEMBLED AT THE VAB (VEHICLE ASSEMBLY BUILDING), A HUGE BUILDING IN THE MIDDLE OF THE KENNEDY SPACE CENTER IN FLORIDA...

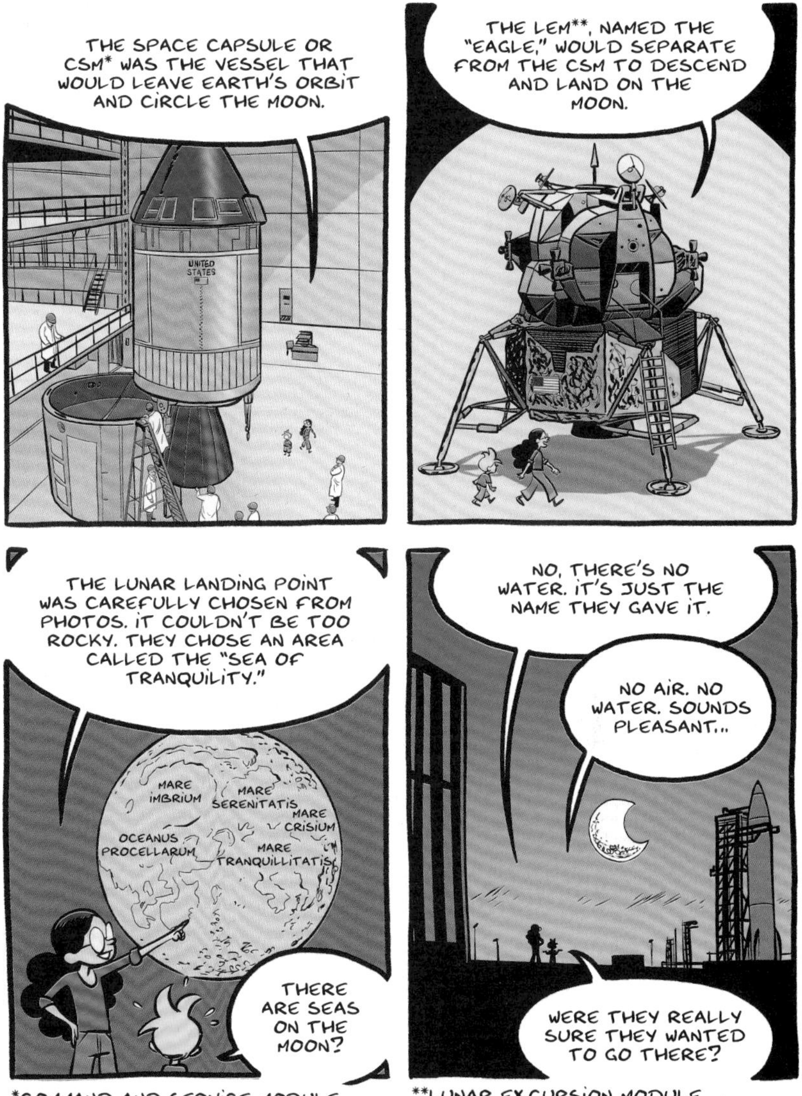
THE SPACE CAPSULE OR CSM* WAS THE VESSEL THAT WOULD LEAVE EARTH'S ORBIT AND CIRCLE THE MOON.
UNITED STATES
THE LEM**, NAMED THE "EAGLE," WOULD SEPARATE FROM THE CSM TO DESCEND AND LAND ON THE MOON.
THE LUNAR LANDING POINT WAS CAREFULLY CHOSEN FROM PHOTOS. IT COULDN'T BE TOO ROCKY. THEY CHOSE AN AREA CALLED THE "SEA OF TRANQUILITY."
MARE IMBRIUM
MARE SERENITATIS
MARE CRISIUM
OCEANUS PROCELLARUM
MARE TRANQUILLITATIS
THERE ARE SEAS ON THE MOON?
NO, THERE'S NO WATER. IT'S JUST THE NAME THEY GAVE IT.
NO AIR. NO WATER. SOUNDS PLEASANT...
WERE THEY REALLY SURE THEY WANTED TO GO THERE?

*COMMAND AND SERVICE MODULE

**LUNAR EXCURSION MODULE

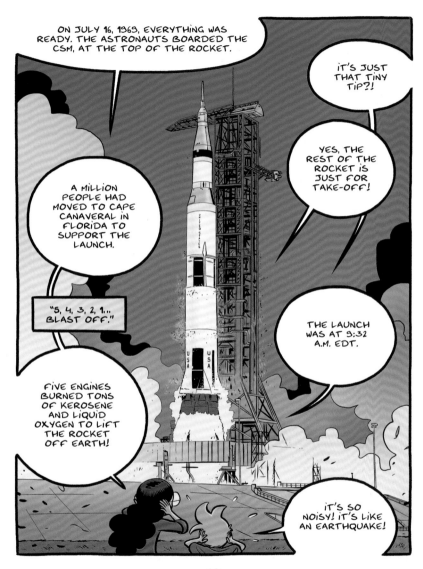

ON JULY 16, 1969, EVERYTHING WAS READY. THE ASTRONAUTS BOARDED THE CSM, AT THE TOP OF THE ROCKET.

IT'S JUST THAT TINY TIP?!

YES, THE REST OF THE ROCKET IS JUST FOR TAKE-OFF!

A MILLION PEOPLE HAD MOVED TO CAPE CANAVERAL IN FLORIDA TO SUPPORT THE LAUNCH.

"5, 4, 3, 2, 1..." BLAST OFF."

THE LAUNCH WAS AT 9:32 A.M. EDT.

FIVE ENGINES BURNED TONS OF KEROSENE AND LIQUID OXYGEN TO LIFT THE ROCKET OFF EARTH!

IT'S SO NOISY! IT'S LIKE AN EARTHQUAKE!

18

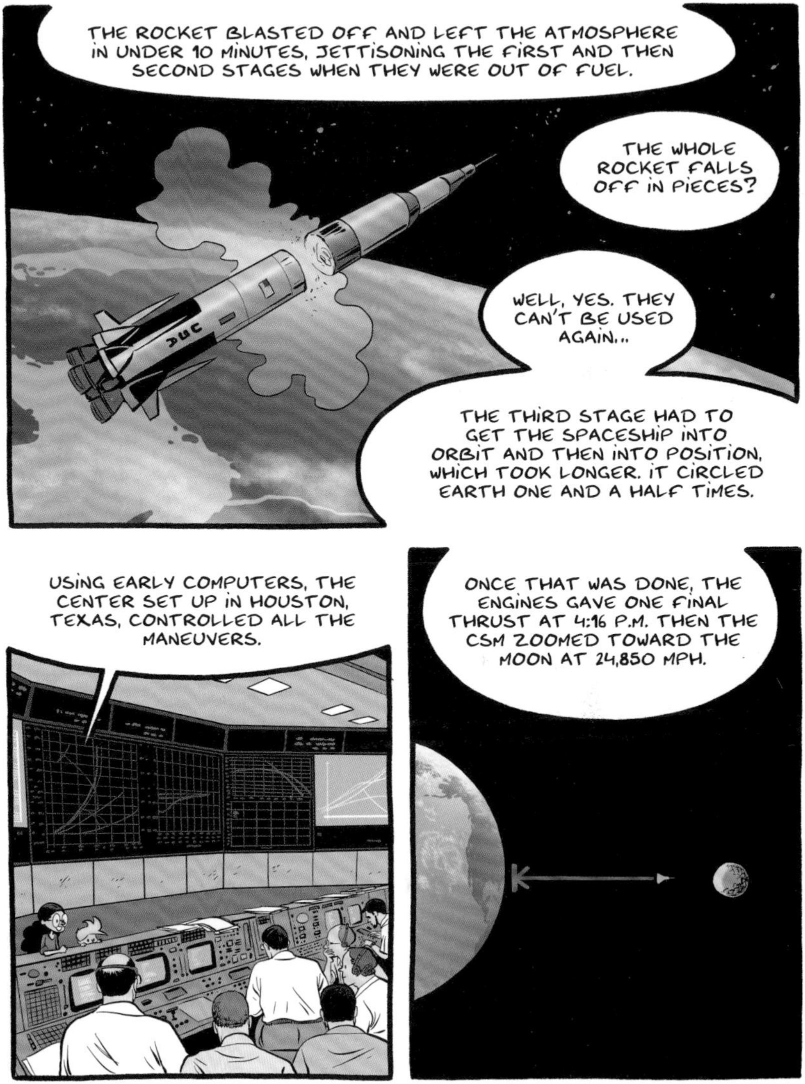
THE ROCKET BLASTED OFF AND LEFT THE ATMOSPHERE IN UNDER 10 MINUTES, JETTISONING THE FIRST AND THEN SECOND STAGES WHEN THEY WERE OUT OF FUEL.
THE WHOLE ROCKET FALLS OFF IN PIECES?
WELL, YES. THEY CAN'T BE USED AGAIN...
THE THIRD STAGE HAD TO GET THE SPACESHIP INTO ORBIT AND THEN INTO POSITION, WHICH TOOK LONGER. IT CIRCLED EARTH ONE AND A HALF TIMES.
USING EARLY COMPUTERS, THE CENTER SET UP IN HOUSTON, TEXAS, CONTROLLED ALL THE MANEUVERS.
ONCE THAT WAS DONE, THE ENGINES GAVE ONE FINAL THRUST AT 4:16 P.M. THEN THE CSM ZOOMED TOWARD THE MOON AT 24,850 MPH.

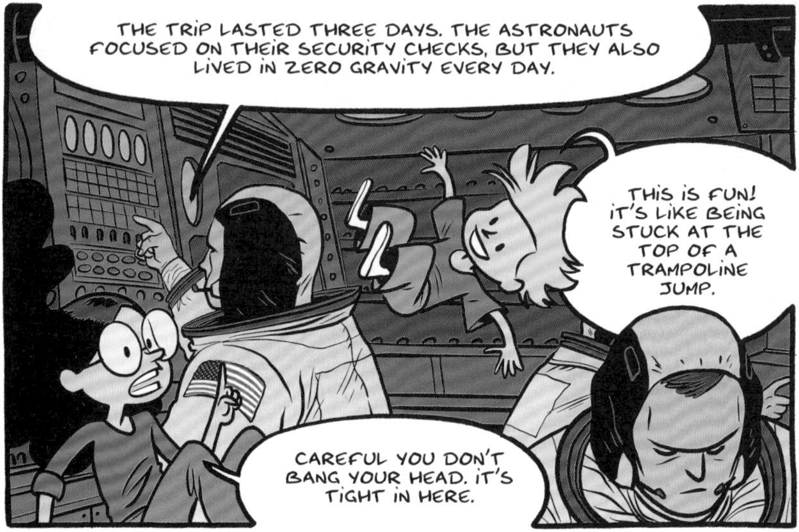
THE TRIP LASTED THREE DAYS. THE ASTRONAUTS FOCUSED ON THEIR SECURITY CHECKS, BUT THEY ALSO LIVED IN ZERO GRAVITY EVERY DAY.
THIS IS FUN! IT'S LIKE BEING STUCK AT THE TOP OF A TRAMPOLINE JUMP.
CAREFUL YOU DON'T BANG YOUR HEAD. IT'S TIGHT IN HERE.

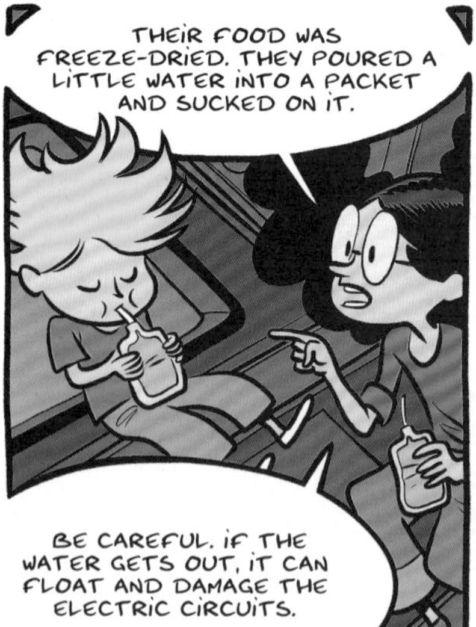
THEIR FOOD WAS FREEZE-DRIED. THEY POURED A LITTLE WATER INTO A PACKET AND SUCKED ON IT.
BE CAREFUL. IF THE WATER GETS OUT, IT CAN FLOAT AND DAMAGE THE ELECTRIC CIRCUITS.

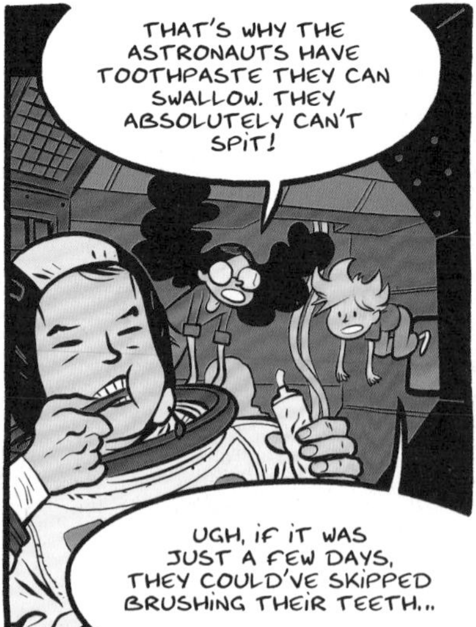
THAT'S WHY THE ASTRONAUTS HAVE TOOTHPASTE THEY CAN SWALLOW. THEY ABSOLUTELY CAN'T SPIT!
UGH, IF IT WAS JUST A FEW DAYS, THEY COULD'VE SKIPPED BRUSHING THEIR TEETH...

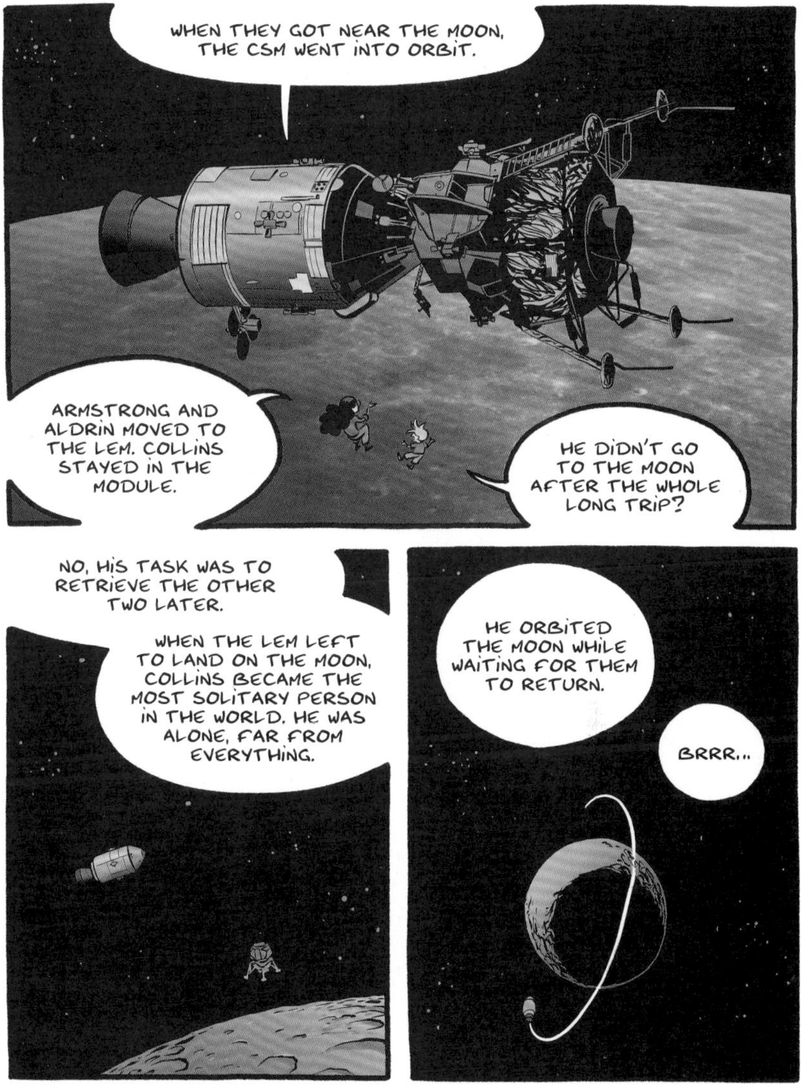
WHEN THEY GOT NEAR THE MOON, THE CSM WENT INTO ORBIT.
ARMSTRONG AND ALDRIN MOVED TO THE LEM. COLLINS STAYED IN THE MODULE.
HE DIDN'T GO TO THE MOON AFTER THE WHOLE LONG TRIP?
NO, HIS TASK WAS TO RETRIEVE THE OTHER TWO LATER.
WHEN THE LEM LEFT TO LAND ON THE MOON, COLLINS BECAME THE MOST SOLITARY PERSON IN THE WORLD. HE WAS ALONE, FAR FROM EVERYTHING.
HE ORBITED THE MOON WHILE WAITING FOR THEM TO RETURN.
BRRR...

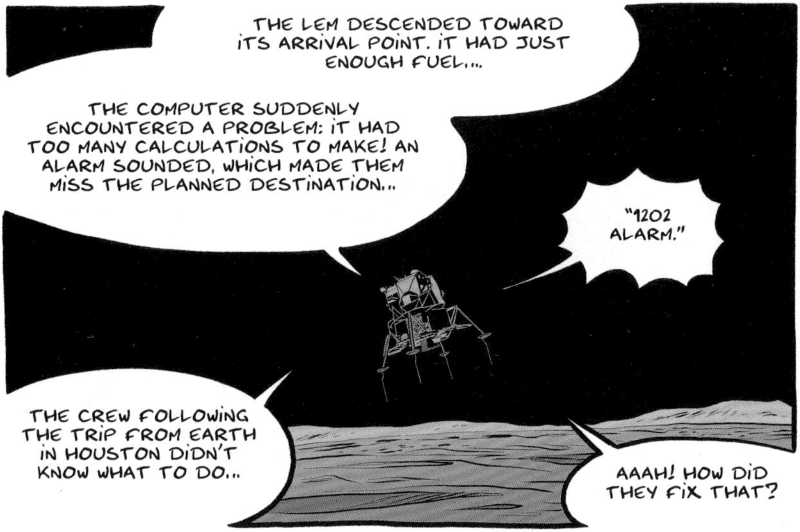
THE LEM DESCENDED TOWARD ITS ARRIVAL POINT. IT HAD JUST ENOUGH FUEL...
THE COMPUTER SUDDENLY ENCOUNTERED A PROBLEM: IT HAD TOO MANY CALCULATIONS TO MAKE! AN ALARM SOUNDED, WHICH MADE THEM MISS THE PLANNED DESTINATION...
"1202 ALARM."
THE CREW FOLLOWING THE TRIP FROM EARTH IN HOUSTON DIDN'T KNOW WHAT TO DO...
AAAH! HOW DID THEY FIX THAT?
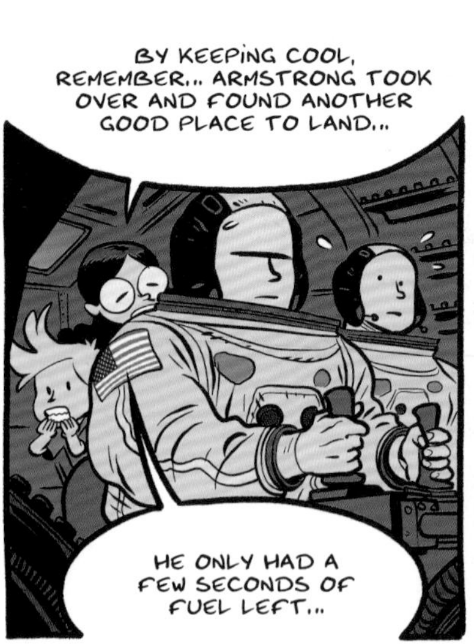
BY KEEPING COOL, REMEMBER... ARMSTRONG TOOK OVER AND FOUND ANOTHER GOOD PLACE TO LAND...
HE ONLY HAD A FEW SECONDS OF FUEL LEFT...
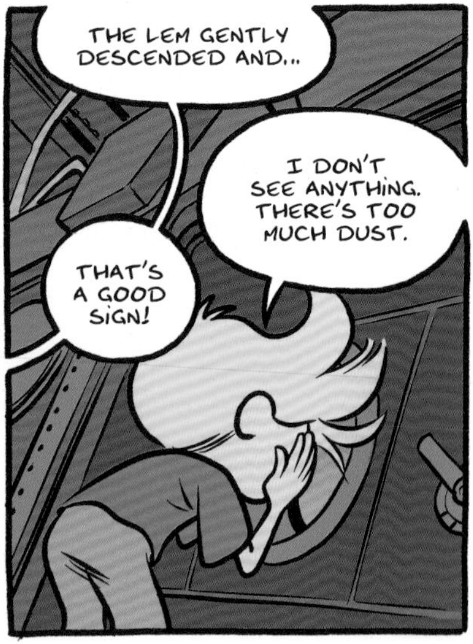
THE LEM GENTLY DESCENDED AND...
I DON'T SEE ANYTHING. THERE'S TOO MUCH DUST.
THAT'S A GOOD SIGN!

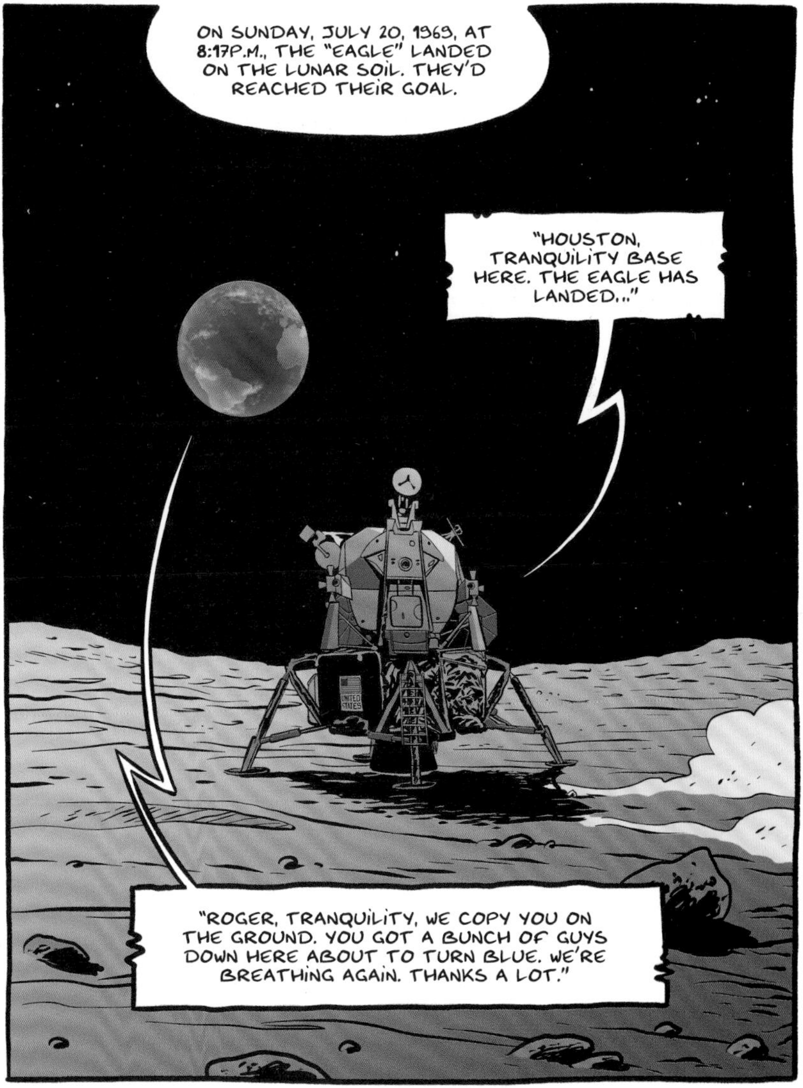
ON SUNDAY, JULY 20, 1969, AT 8:17P.M., THE "EAGLE" LANDED ON THE LUNAR SOIL. THEY'D REACHED THEIR GOAL.
"HOUSTON, TRANQUILITY BASE HERE. THE EAGLE HAS LANDED..."
UNITED STATES
"ROGER, TRANQUILITY, WE COPY YOU ON THE GROUND. YOU GOT A BUNCH OF GUYS DOWN HERE ABOUT TO TURN BLUE. WE'RE BREATHING AGAIN. THANKS A LOT."

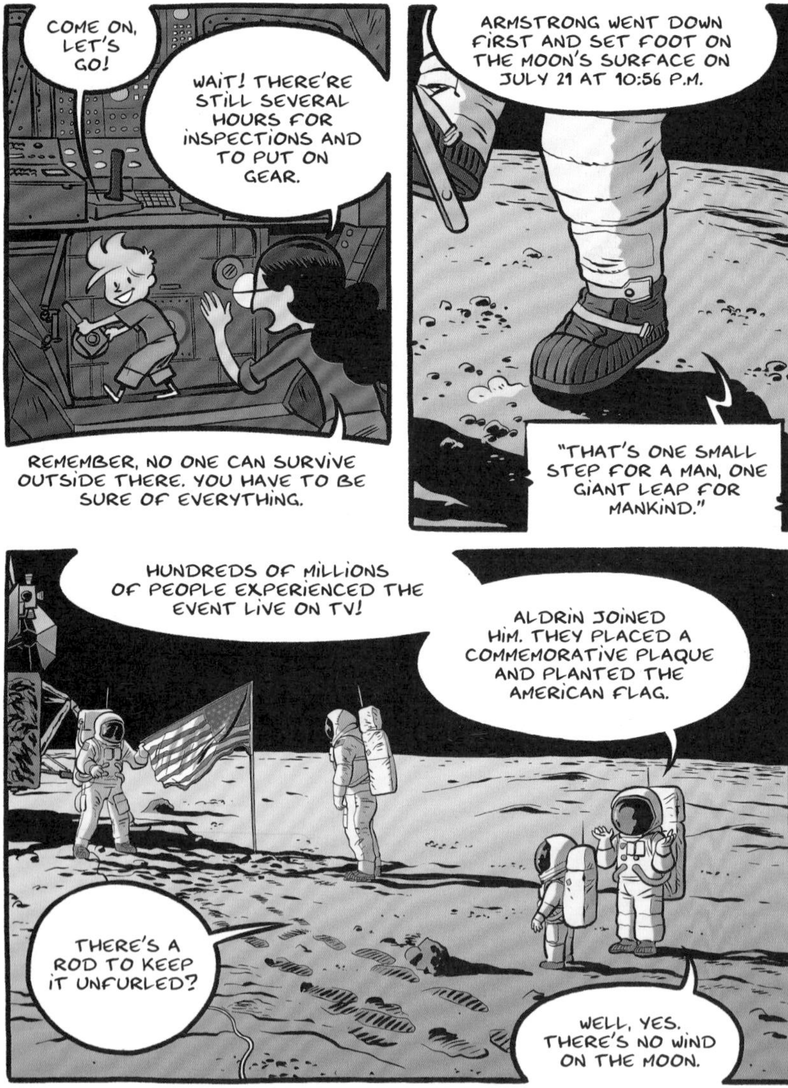

COME ON, LET'S GO!
WAIT! THERE'RE STILL SEVERAL HOURS FOR INSPECTIONS AND TO PUT ON GEAR.
REMEMBER, NO ONE CAN SURVIVE OUTSIDE THERE. YOU HAVE TO BE SURE OF EVERYTHING.
ARMSTRONG WENT DOWN FIRST AND SET FOOT ON THE MOON'S SURFACE ON JULY 21 AT 10:56 P.M.
"THAT'S ONE SMALL STEP FOR A MAN, ONE GIANT LEAP FOR MANKIND."
HUNDREDS OF MILLIONS OF PEOPLE EXPERIENCED THE EVENT LIVE ON TV!
ALDRIN JOINED HIM. THEY PLACED A COMMEMORATIVE PLAQUE AND PLANTED THE AMERICAN FLAG.
THERE'S A ROD TO KEEP IT UNFURLED?
WELL, YES. THERE'S NO WIND ON THE MOON.

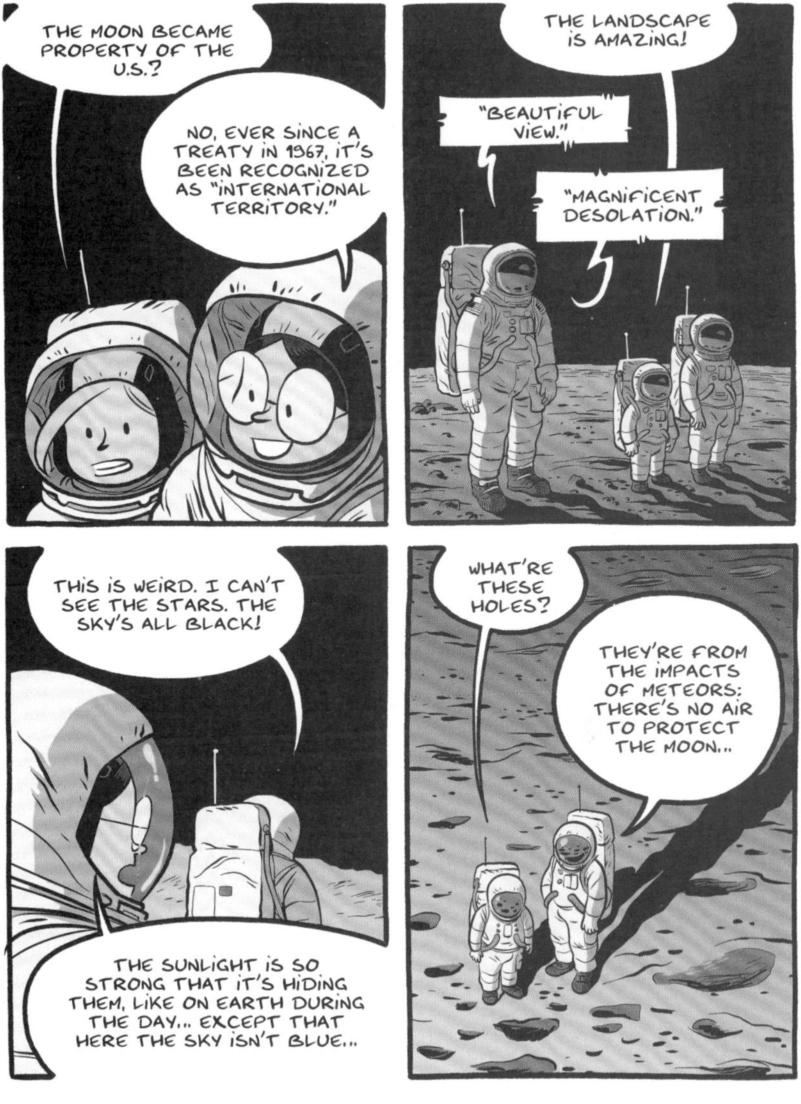
THE MOON BECAME PROPERTY OF THE U.S.?
NO, EVER SINCE A TREATY IN 1967, IT'S BEEN RECOGNIZED AS "INTERNATIONAL TERRITORY."
THE LANDSCAPE IS AMAZING!
"BEAUTIFUL VIEW."
"MAGNIFICENT DESOLATION."
THIS IS WEIRD. I CAN'T SEE THE STARS. THE SKY'S ALL BLACK!
THE SUNLIGHT IS SO STRONG THAT IT'S HIDING THEM, LIKE ON EARTH DURING THE DAY... EXCEPT THAT HERE THE SKY ISN'T BLUE...
WHAT'RE THESE HOLES?
THEY'RE FROM THE IMPACTS OF METEORS: THERE'S NO AIR TO PROTECT THE MOON...

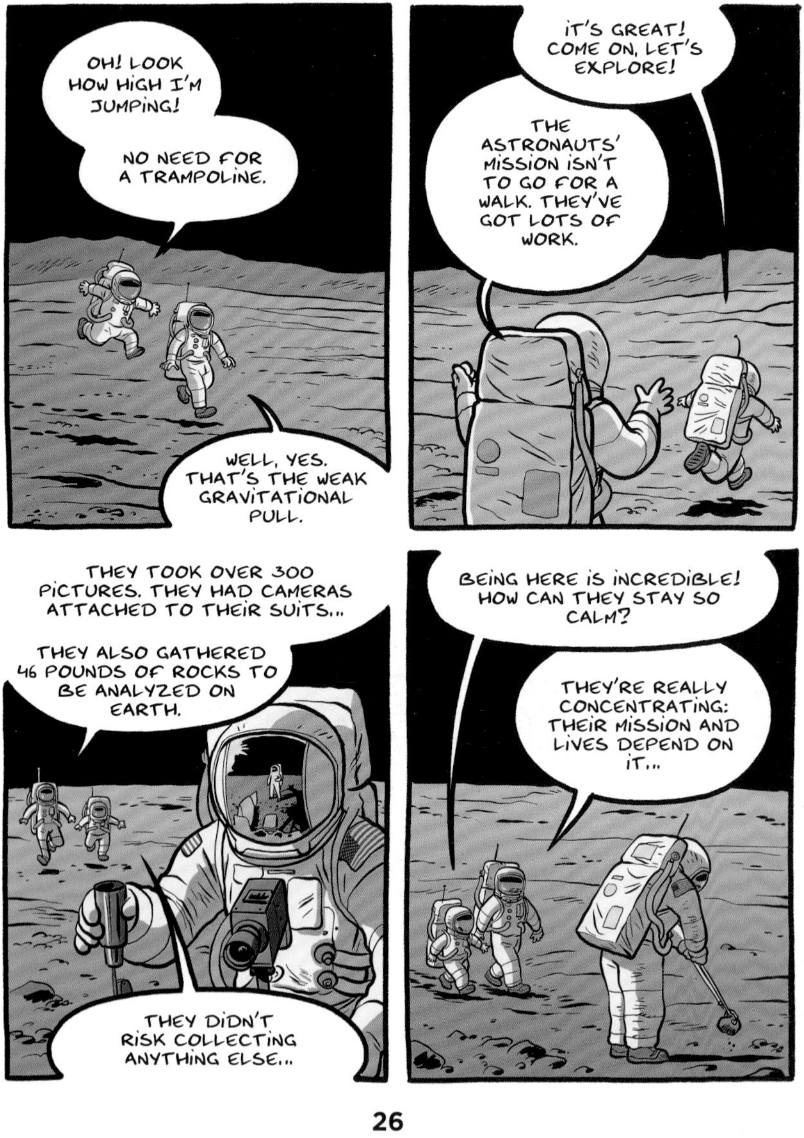
OH! LOOK HOW HIGH I'M JUMPING!
NO NEED FOR A TRAMPOLINE.
WELL, YES. THAT'S THE WEAK GRAVITATIONAL PULL.
IT'S GREAT! COME ON, LET'S EXPLORE!
THE ASTRONAUTS' MISSION ISN'T TO GO FOR A WALK. THEY'VE GOT LOTS OF WORK.
THEY TOOK OVER 300 PICTURES. THEY HAD CAMERAS ATTACHED TO THEIR SUITS...
THEY ALSO GATHERED 46 POUNDS OF ROCKS TO BE ANALYZED ON EARTH.
THEY DIDN'T RISK COLLECTING ANYTHING ELSE...
BEING HERE IS INCREDIBLE! HOW CAN THEY STAY SO CALM?
THEY'RE REALLY CONCENTRATING: THEIR MISSION AND LIVES DEPEND ON IT...

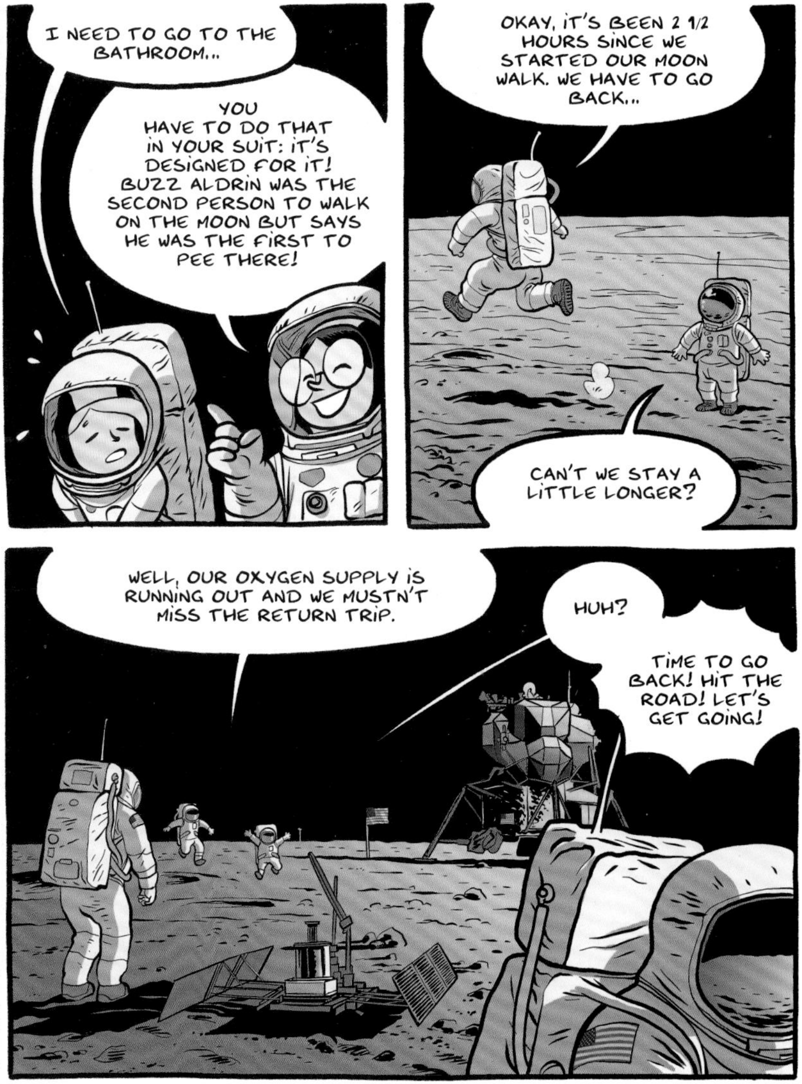
I NEED TO GO TO THE BATHROOM...
YOU HAVE TO DO THAT IN YOUR SUIT: IT'S DESIGNED FOR IT! BUZZ ALDRIN WAS THE SECOND PERSON TO WALK ON THE MOON BUT SAYS HE WAS THE FIRST TO PEE THERE!
OKAY, IT'S BEEN 2 1/2 HOURS SINCE WE STARTED OUR MOON WALK. WE HAVE TO GO BACK...
CAN'T WE STAY A LITTLE LONGER?
WELL, OUR OXYGEN SUPPLY IS RUNNING OUT AND WE MUSTN'T MISS THE RETURN TRIP.
HUH?
TIME TO GO BACK! HIT THE ROAD! LET'S GET GOING!

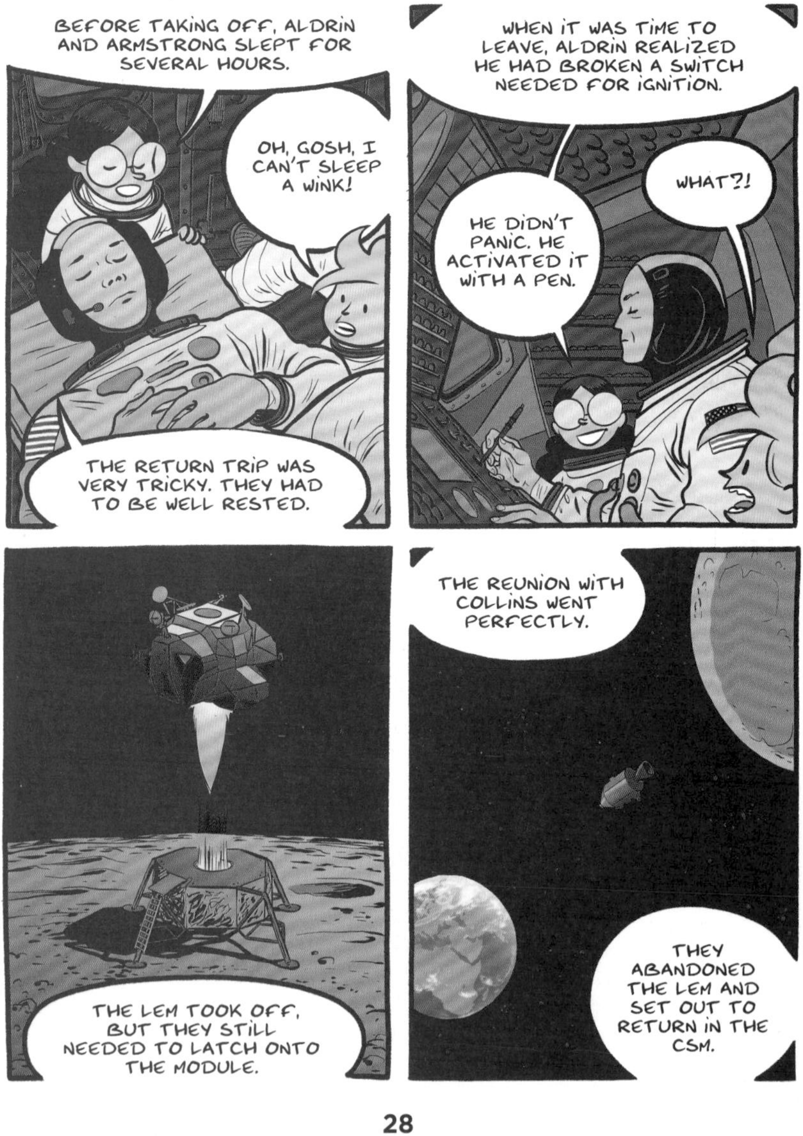
BEFORE TAKING OFF, ALDRIN AND ARMSTRONG SLEPT FOR SEVERAL HOURS.
OH, GOSH, I CAN'T SLEEP A WINK!
THE RETURN TRIP WAS VERY TRICKY. THEY HAD TO BE WELL RESTED.
WHEN IT WAS TIME TO LEAVE, ALDRIN REALIZED HE HAD BROKEN A SWITCH NEEDED FOR IGNITION.
WHAT?!
HE DIDN'T PANIC. HE ACTIVATED IT WITH A PEN.
THE LEM TOOK OFF, BUT THEY STILL NEEDED TO LATCH ONTO THE MODULE.
THE REUNION WITH COLLINS WENT PERFECTLY.
THEY ABANDONED THE LEM AND SET OUT TO RETURN IN THE CSM.

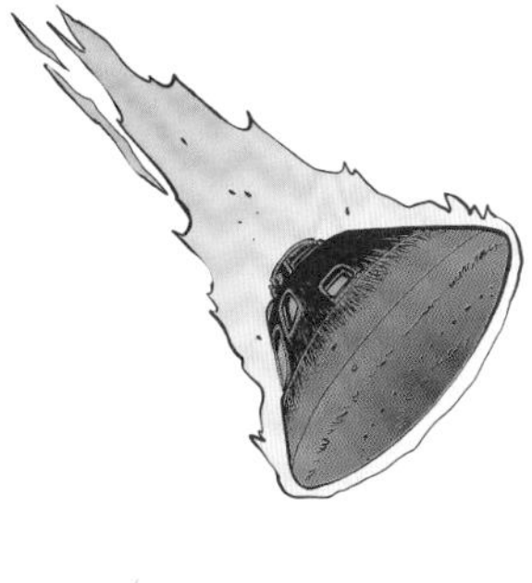

ON JULY 24, 1969, THEY REENTERED EARTH'S ATMOSPHERE. THE SHOCK WAS VIOLENT: AT THE SPEED THEY WERE TRAVELING, THE AIR AROUND THEM CAUGHT FIRE!

THE TRIP ENDED (AS PLANNED) IN THE PACIFIC OCEAN. THE ASTRONAUTS WERE RETRIEVED SAFE AND SOUND.

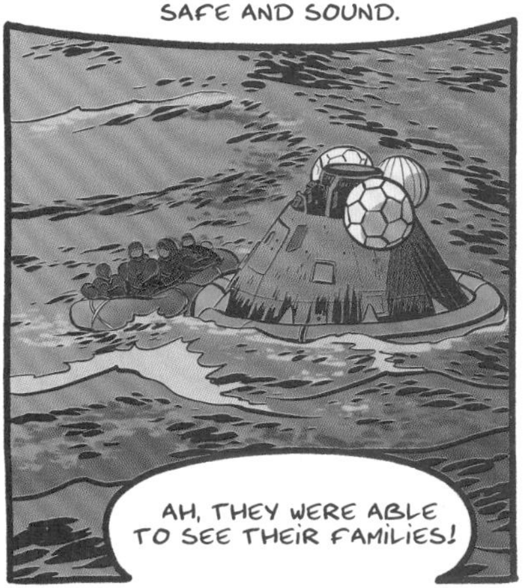
AH, THEY WERE ABLE TO SEE THEIR FAMILIES!

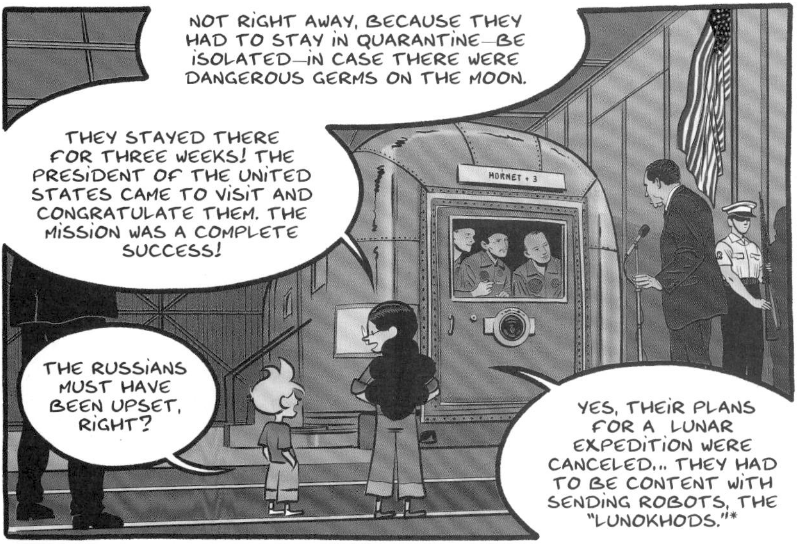
NOT RIGHT AWAY, BECAUSE THEY HAD TO STAY IN QUARANTINE—BE ISOLATED—IN CASE THERE WERE DANGEROUS GERMS ON THE MOON.
THEY STAYED THERE FOR THREE WEEKS! THE PRESIDENT OF THE UNITED STATES CAME TO VISIT AND CONGRATULATE THEM. THE MISSION WAS A COMPLETE SUCCESS!
HORNET + 3
THE RUSSIANS MUST HAVE BEEN UPSET, RIGHT?
YES, THEIR PLANS FOR A LUNAR EXPEDITION WERE CANCELED... THEY HAD TO BE CONTENT WITH SENDING ROBOTS, THE "LUNOKHODS."*

*"MOONWALKERS" IN RUSSIAN.

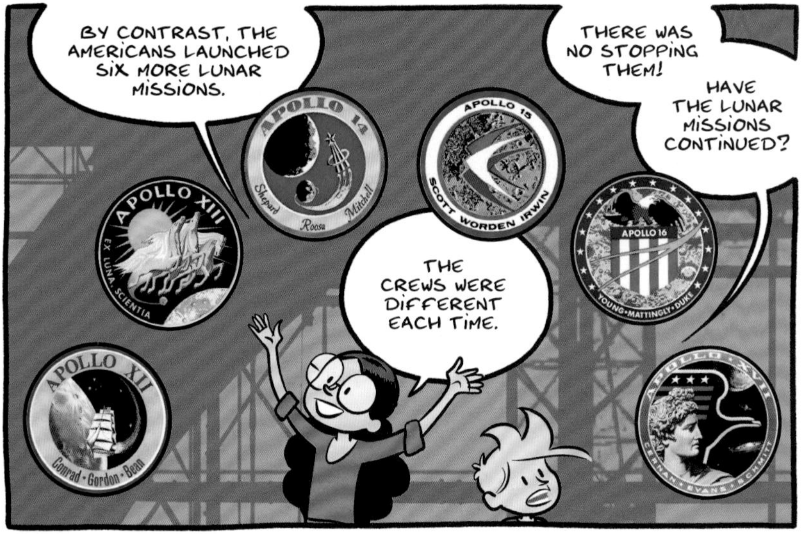
BY CONTRAST, THE AMERICANS LAUNCHED SIX MORE LUNAR MISSIONS.
THERE WAS NO STOPPING THEM!
HAVE THE LUNAR MISSIONS CONTINUED?
APOLLO 14
Shepard Roosa Mitchell
APOLLO 15
SCOTT WORDEN IRWIN
APOLLO XIII
EX LUNA, SCIENTIA
APOLLO 16
YOUNG·MATTINGLY·DUKE
APOLLO XII
Conrad · Gordon · Bean
THE CREWS WERE DIFFERENT EACH TIME.

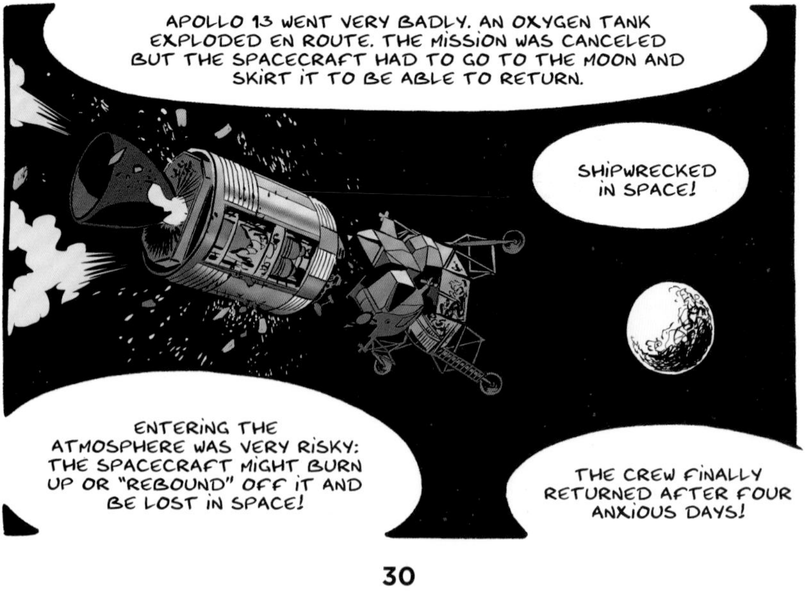
APOLLO 13 WENT VERY BADLY. AN OXYGEN TANK EXPLODED EN ROUTE. THE MISSION WAS CANCELED BUT THE SPACECRAFT HAD TO GO TO THE MOON AND SKIRT IT TO BE ABLE TO RETURN.
SHIPWRECKED IN SPACE!
ENTERING THE ATMOSPHERE WAS VERY RISKY: THE SPACECRAFT MIGHT BURN UP OR "REBOUND" OFF IT AND BE LOST IN SPACE!
THE CREW FINALLY RETURNED AFTER FOUR ANXIOUS DAYS!

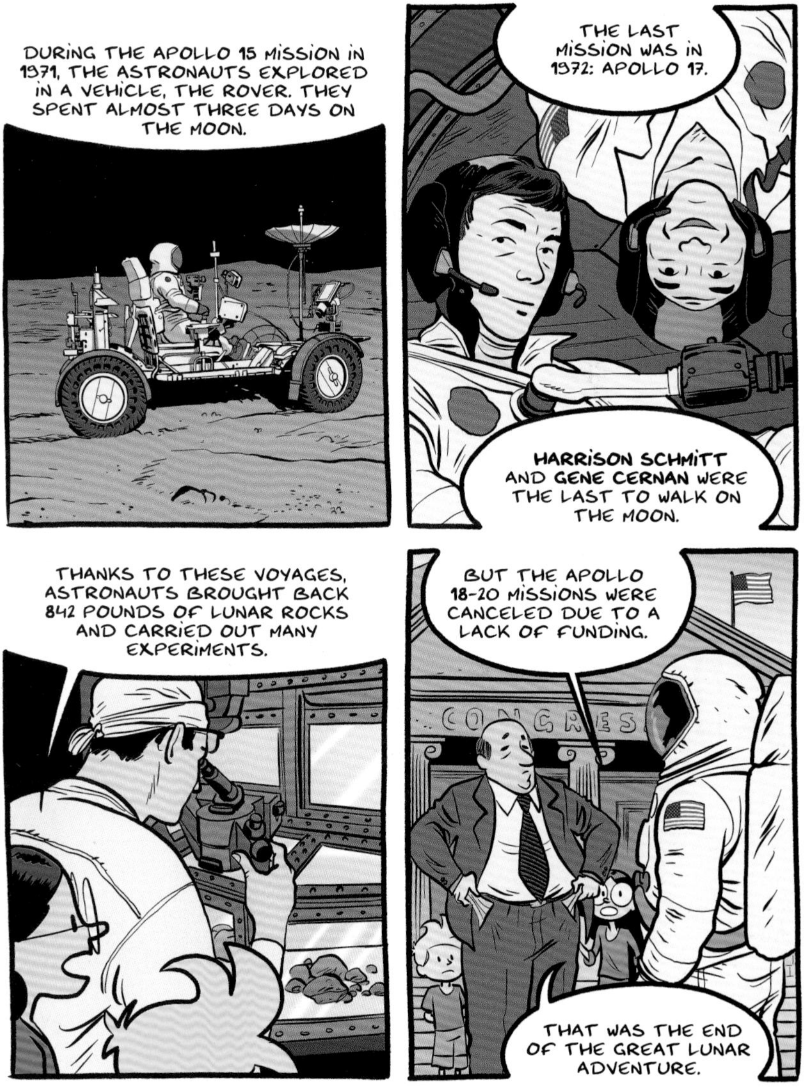
DURING THE APOLLO 15 MISSION IN 1971, THE ASTRONAUTS EXPLORED IN A VEHICLE, THE ROVER. THEY SPENT ALMOST THREE DAYS ON THE MOON.
THE LAST MISSION WAS IN 1972: APOLLO 17.
HARRISON SCHMITT AND GENE CERNAN WERE THE LAST TO WALK ON THE MOON.
THANKS TO THESE VOYAGES, ASTRONAUTS BROUGHT BACK 842 POUNDS OF LUNAR ROCKS AND CARRIED OUT MANY EXPERIMENTS.
BUT THE APOLLO 18-20 MISSIONS WERE CANCELED DUE TO A LACK OF FUNDING.
CONGRES
THAT WAS THE END OF THE GREAT LUNAR ADVENTURE.

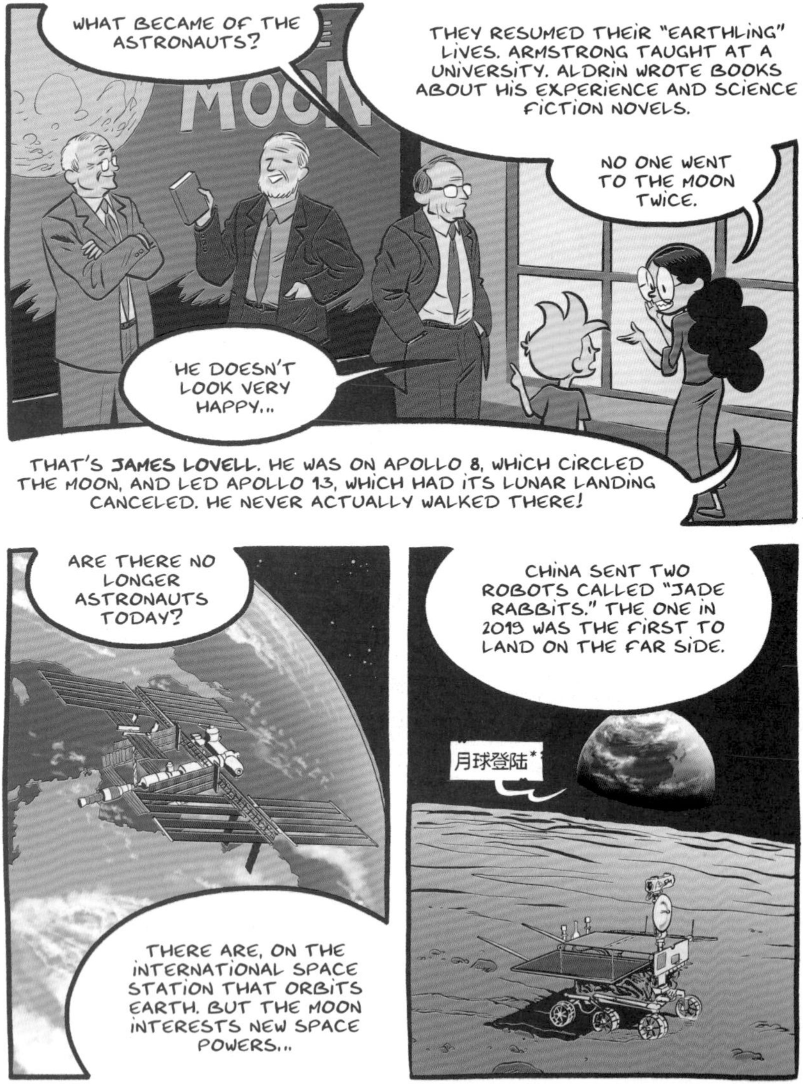
MOON
WHAT BECAME OF THE ASTRONAUTS?
THEY RESUMED THEIR "EARTHLING" LIVES. ARMSTRONG TAUGHT AT A UNIVERSITY. ALDRIN WROTE BOOKS ABOUT HIS EXPERIENCE AND SCIENCE FICTION NOVELS.
NO ONE WENT TO THE MOON TWICE.
HE DOESN'T LOOK VERY HAPPY...
THAT'S **JAMES LOVELL**. HE WAS ON APOLLO 8, WHICH CIRCLED THE MOON, AND LED APOLLO 13, WHICH HAD ITS LUNAR LANDING CANCELED. HE NEVER ACTUALLY WALKED THERE!
ARE THERE NO LONGER ASTRONAUTS TODAY?
THERE ARE, ON THE INTERNATIONAL SPACE STATION THAT ORBITS EARTH. BUT THE MOON INTERESTS NEW SPACE POWERS...
CHINA SENT TWO ROBOTS CALLED "JADE RABBITS." THE ONE IN 2019 WAS THE FIRST TO LAND ON THE FAR SIDE.
月球登陆*

*MOON LANDING.

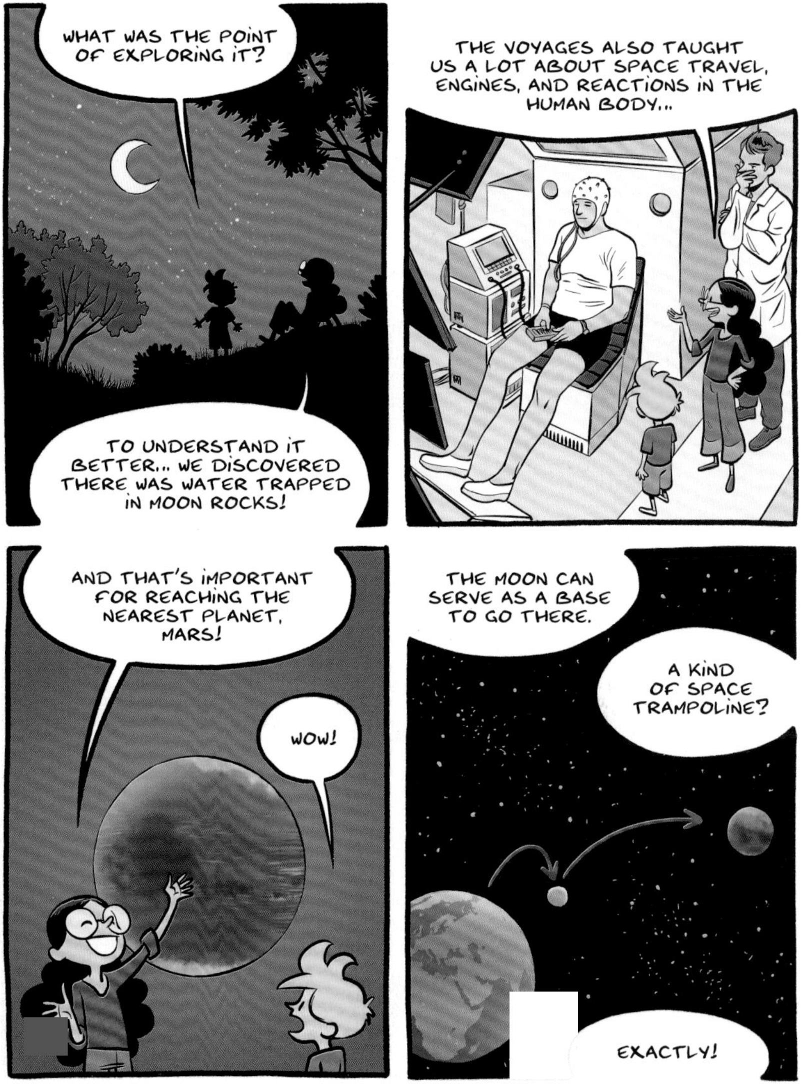
WHAT WAS THE POINT OF EXPLORING IT?
TO UNDERSTAND IT BETTER... WE DISCOVERED THERE WAS WATER TRAPPED IN MOON ROCKS!
THE VOYAGES ALSO TAUGHT US A LOT ABOUT SPACE TRAVEL, ENGINES, AND REACTIONS IN THE HUMAN BODY...
AND THAT'S IMPORTANT FOR REACHING THE NEAREST PLANET, MARS!
WOW!
THE MOON CAN SERVE AS A BASE TO GO THERE.
A KIND OF SPACE TRAMPOLINE?
EXACTLY!

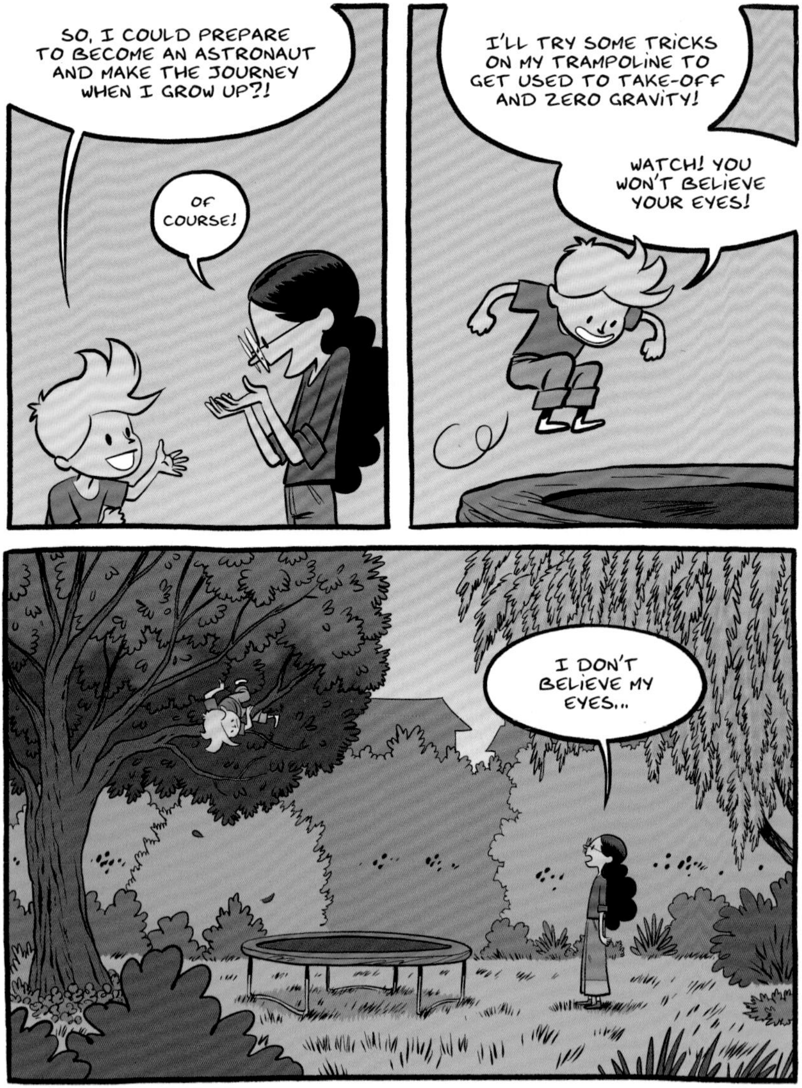
SO, I COULD PREPARE TO BECOME AN ASTRONAUT AND MAKE THE JOURNEY WHEN I GROW UP?!
OF COURSE!
I'LL TRY SOME TRICKS ON MY TRAMPOLINE TO GET USED TO TAKE-OFF AND ZERO GRAVITY!
WATCH! YOU WON'T BELIEVE YOUR EYES!
I DON'T BELIEVE MY EYES...

AND THERE'S MORE...

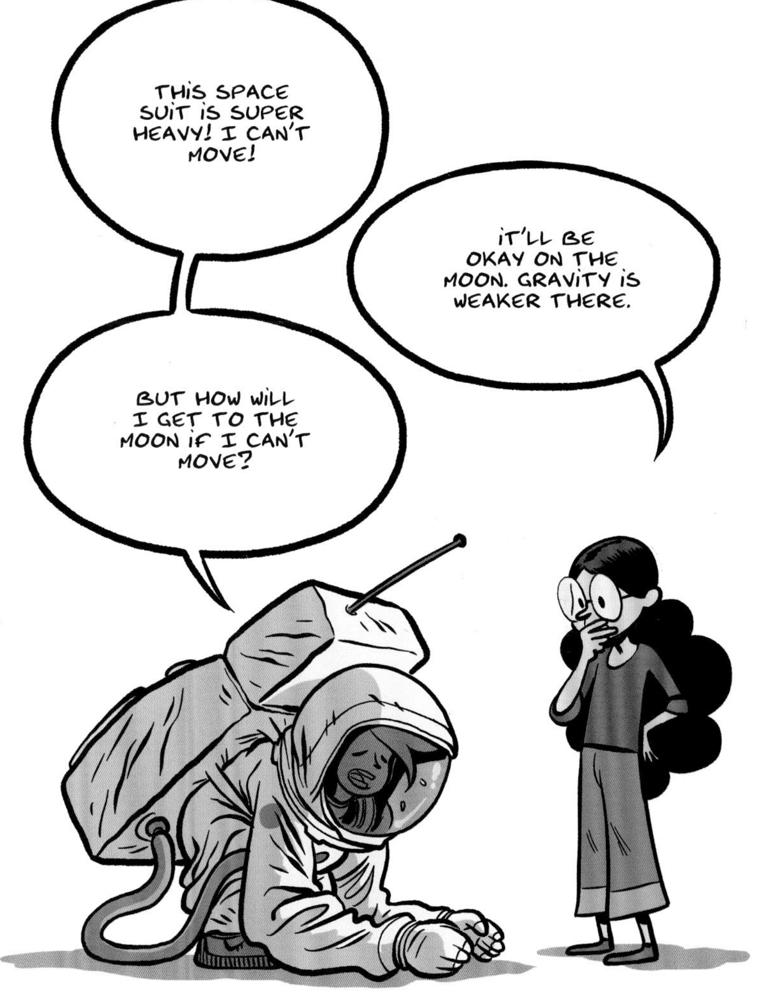
THIS SPACE SUIT IS SUPER HEAVY! I CAN'T MOVE!
IT'LL BE OKAY ON THE MOON. GRAVITY IS WEAKER THERE.
BUT HOW WILL I GET TO THE MOON IF I CAN'T MOVE?

Some People Who Made History

Neil Armstrong
(1930-2012)

Armstrong earned a degree in aeronautical engineering. A test pilot for the National Advisory Committee for Aeronautics (NACA) he tried out new machines—rocket-planes. In 1962, he was chosen in the second group of astronauts that NASA trained. Commander of the Gemini 8 mission in 1966, he docked two vessels in space. He was next selected to command the Apollo 11 mission and became the first man to walk on the moon. Shortly after the mission, he left NASA and became a professor.

Edwin Aldrin (a.k.a. Buzz)
(b. 1930)

A military pilot during the Korean War (1950-53), Aldrin studied astronautics afterward. In 1963, he was admitted in the third group of astronauts NASA trained. During the Gemini 12 mission in 1966, he went outside the spacecraft into space (called an EVA— Extra Vehicular Activity) He was chosen to pilot the LEM during the Apollo 11 mission and became the second man to walk on the moon. He inspired the character of Buzz Lightyear in Toy Story in 1995.

Christopher Kraft
(1924-2019)

An American engineer, Kraft specialized in aerospace engineering and was part of the first team that worked at NASA to send men into space. He became the flight director for the Mercury and Gemini missions and supervised all the activities. He set up and organized the Mission Control system that guided the astronauts from the Earth. He then planned the Apollo missions but left the role of flight director to Gene Kranz.

Katherine Johnson
(1918-2020)

An American mathematician, Johnson was hired in 1953 as part of the group of women responsible for verifying calculations made by the aeronautics agency (NACA—National Advisory Committee for Aeronautics, the predecessor to NASA) and then NASA. She helped calculate the trajectories of numerous space missions: for Apollo 11, she worked on the return of the LEM to the CSM after it left the moon, a rendezvous that couldn't be missed! She was one of the few women to have been associated with the program.

The Most Powerful Rocket in the World

Weighing 6.2 million pounds and 363 feet tall, the **Saturn V launch vehicle** was developed by the U.S. and could propel the Apollo astronaut crews beyond Earth's gravitational pull. It was a multi-stage rocket, with each stage playing a role.

The Saturn V rocket was assembled in a **526-foot-tall hangar** located at the Kennedy Space Center in Florida (in the southeastern United States).

The rocket was then transported to the launchpad by a "crawler," a **tracked vehicle weighing 6.6 million pounds**. It was very slow and took 6 hours to cover 4.3 miles.

The rocket was connected to a **465-foot tall umbilical tower**, which allowed the three stages to be fueled and the astronauts to reach the top—where they had to be.

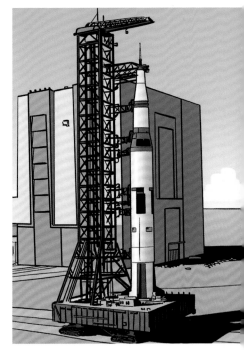

During blastoff, the nine "arms" that linked the rocket to the tower retracted: then the rocket was released!

1 The **safety tower** (33 ft. long) is a launch escape system that lets the CSM be evacuated in case of accidents during launch.

2 The **CSM** is the module where the astronauts are. The cone-shaped portion is the only part that returns to the Earth at the end of the mission.

3 The **LEM**, which is integrated in the rocket, is extracted by the CSM once in orbit, in order to go to the moon.

4 The **third stage** (58 feet long) carries 291,000 pounds of fuel (liquid hydrogen and oxygen). It burns for nearly three minutes to enter Earth's orbit and for five minutes for going to the moon.

5 The **second stage** (82 feet long) consumes over 882 pounds of liquid hydrogen and oxygen in the six minutes of flight to reach the upper layers of the atmosphere.

6 The **first stage** (138 feet long) is propelled by five engines. It burns 4,410 pounds of fuel (kerosene and liquid oxygen) in 2 1/2 minutes, allowing the entire assembly to lift off from the Earth. Flames 164 feet long come out of it!

It takes 134 tanker trucks to fill the rocket with fuel!

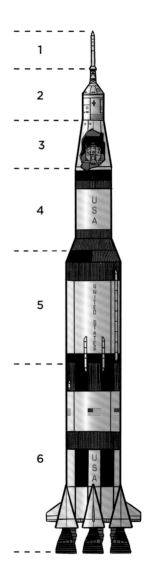

The Apollo Mission Modules

The spacecraft that the astronauts traveled in were very cramped: every available spot had to be used for propulsion (engines, fuel, etc.), the astronauts' survival (oxygen, heat shield for the heat when reentering the atmosphere, etc.), and guidance (telescope, control levers, etc.).

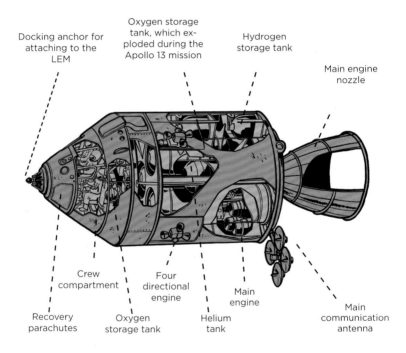

Docking anchor for attaching to the LEM

Oxygen storage tank, which exploded during the Apollo 13 mission

Hydrogen storage tank

Main engine nozzle

Recovery parachutes

Crew compartment

Oxygen storage tank

Four directional engine

Helium tank

Main engine

Main communication antenna

COMMAND SERVICE MODULE (CSM)

ASCENT STAGE

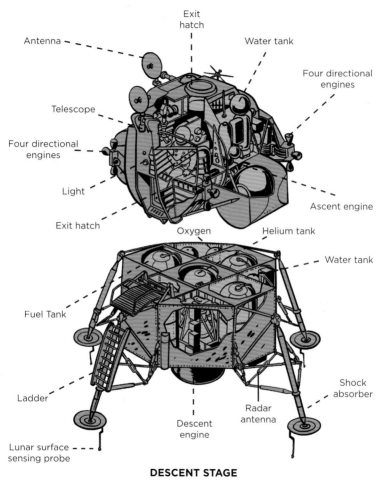

Exit hatch

Antenna

Water tank

Four directional engines

Telescope

Four directional engines

Light

Ascent engine

Exit hatch

Oxygen

Helium tank

Water tank

Fuel Tank

Ladder

Shock absorber

Radar antenna

Descent engine

Lunar surface sensing probe

DESCENT STAGE

Lunar Module (LEM)

Timeline

The Germans develop V2 missiles, which serve as the basis for space rockets.

▼

1942

The Russians and Americans get the German scientists to develop their program.

▼

1945

July 1969

▲

Two men walk on the moon for the first time on the Apollo 11 mission.

1968

▲

Three astronauts circle the moon on the American Apollo 8 mission.

1970

▲

The Apollo 13 mission is forced to return to Earth due to an accident.

1972

▲

Apollo 17 is the last lunar mission in the program.

The Russians send the Sputnik satellite and then the dog Laika into orbit.

▼

The Russian Yuri Gagarin is the first man to fly in space.

▼

1957

April 1961

1965

1961

▲

▲

The Russian Alexei Leonov takes the first extra-vehicular spacewalk.

The U.S. President John F. Kennedy commits to having a man walk on the moon in under ten years.

2013

2019

▲

▲

The Chinese send a to the moon.

A second Jade Rabbit moon for the first time.

WATCH OUT FOR PAPERCUTZ ™

Welcome to the tenth totally thrilling MAGICAL HISTORY TOUR graphic novel, featuring the fantastic fact-filled story of the "First Steps on the Moon: The Apollo Project," written by Fabrice Erre and illustrated by Sylvain Savoia and brought to you by Papercutz, those spacey folks dedicated to publishing great graphic novels for all ages. I'm Jim Salicrup, the Editor-in-Chief and 108,223,904,575th Person to Step on the Earth, here to ponder some thoughts about the mission to the moon.

We're living in somewhat cynical times, where people are often questioning what they're told. While it's a good thing not to believe whatever you hear without supporting facts to back it up, sometimes people can make up fantastic stories to explain what "really" happened. Case in point, man walking on the moon. This seems so unbelievable to some people that they are convinced it never happened. They believe it was all faked, filmed in a film studio.

It reminds me of something that happened years before the moon landing, on October 30, 1938, the brilliant actor, writer, director Orson Welles produced a radio drama based on the classic novel "War of the Worlds," by H.G. Wells (no relation). To make his adaptation of the novel as exciting as possible, it was treated as if it was an actual news broadcast, and some listeners believed it was true—that we were being invaded by Martians. But that really was a fictional presentation, the moon-landing, at least in my opinion, was real.

Despite all the science involved with sending a man to the moon, it essentially came down to putting some guys in a big tin can with a big rocket under it. I still get nervous flying in a jet plane, I can't imagine how scary it had to be to take a rocket to the moon. It could've been a nightmare—so many things could've gone wrong. The rocket could've blown up. The spacecraft could've malfunctioned in so many ways—leaving them stranded in space or on the moon. If that happened there would've been no way to rescue them. Fortunately, they were able to go to the moon and come back alive.

I was just 12 years old back in 1969, and I was a fascinated with every detail of this awesome adventure. My family and I sat transfixed in front of our TV set as we watched history happening before our eyes. From the countdown to the splash-down, it was incredibly thrilling. I fondly remember sending away through the mail for a book about the Apollo mission, that came with a tiny toy model of the Lunar Module.

During the '60s the Space Race had a huge impact on pop culture. One could fill a huge book simply listing the TV shows, movies, comicbooks, etc., that were all inspired by the quest to get to the moon. From *Star Trek* to *Lost in Space*, to *2001: A Space Odyssey* to *Planet of the Apes*, to *The Fantastic Four* to *The Amazing Spider-Man*, everyone was suddenly space-crazy. Speaking of pop culture, in the classic comedy sit-com, Jackie Gleason's character, Ralph Kramden, with often "jokingly" threaten his wife with, "One of the these days, Alice…Pow! To the moon!" It was a different time then, and while there were women astronauts later on, only men made it to the moon.

While this graphic novel mainly focuses on Neil Armstrong (1930-2012) and Edwin "Buzz" Aldrin (1930), let's not forget the other ten men who walked on the moon:

- Charles "Pete" Conrad (1930-1999)— Apollo 12
- Alan Bean (1932-2018)—Apollo 12
- Alan B. Shepard Jr. (1923-1998)—Apollo 14
- Edgar D. Mitchell (1930-2016)—Apollo 14
- David R. Scott (1932-)—Apollo 15
- James B. Irwin (1930-1991)—Apollo 15
- John W. Young (1930-2018)—Apollo 10 (orbital), Apollo 16 (landing)
- Charles M. Duke (1935-)—Apollo 16
- Eugene Cernan (1934-2017)—Apollo 10 (orbital), Apollo 17 (landing)
- Harrison H. Schmitt (1935-)—Apollo 17

One final fun fact: William Shatner, the actor famed for playing Captain Kirk on *Star Trek*, finally flew into space for real (for about three minutes) on October 13, 2021, becoming, at age 90, the oldest person to ever travel into space.

While telling fact from fiction can be tricky at times, let our fictional friends, Annie and Nico, continue to offer up more facts in MAGICAL MYSTERY TOUR #11, coming soon to your favorite bookseller or library. And that's a fact!

Thanks,

JIM

STAY IN TOUCH!

EMAIL: salicrup@papercutz.com
WEB: www.papercutz.com
TWITTER: @papercutzgn
INSTAGRAM: @papercutz
FACEBOOK: PAPERCUTZGRAPHICNOVELS
FANMAIL: Papercutz, 160 Broadway, Suite 700, East Wing, New York, NY 10038

Go to papercutz.com and sign up for the free Papercutz e-newsletter!

Fabrice Erre has a Ph.D. in History and teaches Geography and History at the Lycée Jean Jaures near Montpellier, France. He has written a thesis on the satirical press, writes the blog *Une anne au lycée (A Year in High School)* on the website of *Le Monde*, one of France's top national newspapers, and has published several comics.

Sylvain Savoia draws the *Marzi* series, which tells the history of Poland as seen through the eyes of a child. He has also drawn *Les Esclaves oubliés de Tromelin (The Forgotten Slaves of Tromelin)*, which won the *Academie de Marine de Paris* prize.

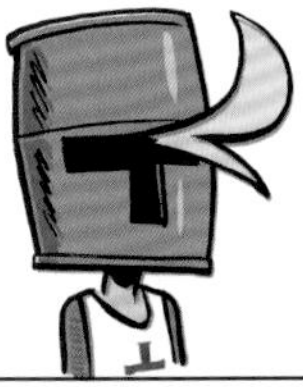

WHERE WILL THE MAGICAL HISTORY TOUR BRING ANNIE AND NICO NEXT?

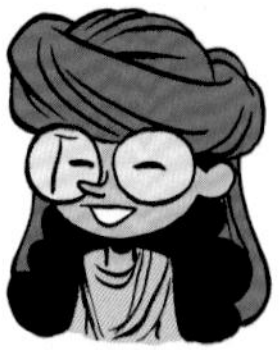

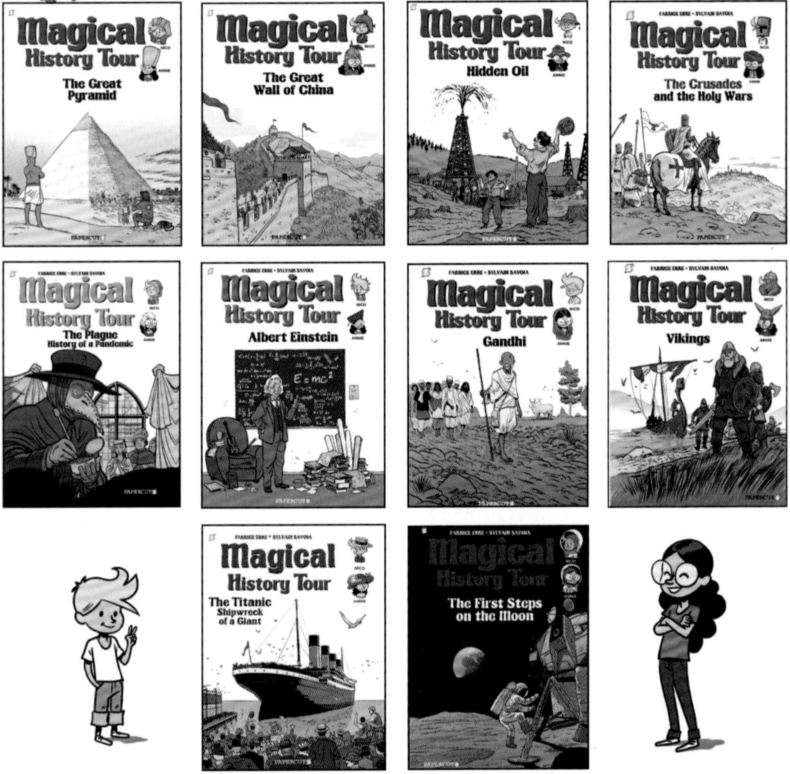
Magical History Tour
The Great Pyramid
Magical History Tour
The Great Wall of China
Magical History Tour
Hidden Oil
Magical History Tour
The Crusades and the Holy Wars
Magical History Tour
The Plague
History of a Pandemic
Magical History Tour
Albert Einstein
Magical History Tour
Gandhi
Magical History Tour
Vikings
Magical History Tour
The Titanic
Shipwreck of a Giant
Magical History Tour
The First Steps on the Moon

MAGICAL HISTORY TOUR graphic novels are available in hardcover only for $6.99 each at booksellers everywhere. Order online at www.papercutz.com.
Or call 1-800-886-1223,
Monday through Friday, 9 – 5 EST. MC, Visa, and AmEx accepted.
To order by mail, please add $5.00 for postage and handling for first book ordered, $1.00 for each additional book and make check payable to NBM Publishing.
Send to: Papercutz, 160 Broadway, Suite 700, East Wing, New York, NY 10038.
MAGICAL HISTORY TOUR graphic novels are also available digitally wherever e-books are sold.